Stadium Stories:

Texas Longhorns

Stadium Stories™ Series

Stadium Stories:
Texas Longhorns

Bill Little

INSIDERS' GUIDE ®

GUILFORD, CONNECTICUT
AN IMPRINT OF THE GLOBE PEQUOT PRESS

INSIDERS' GUIDE®

Copyright © 2005 by The Globe Pequot Press

Text design: Casey Shain
All photos are courtesy of the University of Texas Sports Photography archives, except where noted.
Cover photos: *front cover:* Dusty Mangum (Susan Sigmon); *back cover:* top, "Doc Henry" Reeves; bottom, Darrell K Royal–Texas Memorial Stadium.

Library of Congress Cataloging-in-Publication Data
Little, Bill, 1942-
    Stadium stories : Texas Longhorns / Bill Little. — 1st ed.
        p. cm. — (Stadium stories series)
    ISBN 0-7627-3807-3
1. University of Texas at Austin—Football—History. 2. Texas Longhorns (Football team)—History. I. Title: Texas Longhorns. II. Title. III. Series.

GV958.T4L58 2005
796.332'63'0976431—dc22   2005046218

Manufactured in the United States of America
First Edition/Second Printing

For Ruth and Eddie.

Contents

Acknowledgments

To appropriately acknowledge contributors to this book, we must place them in two categories: those who made history, and those who had the foresight to chronicle it.

First, thanks to Lou Maysel, my first boss at the *Austin American Statesman* and author of *Here Come the Texas Longhorns*. Lou's research made telling stories of the early days really easy.

Second, thanks to the Texas Sports Information Office. Three men—Bill Sansing, Wilbur Evans, and Jones Ramsey—were primarily responsible for preserving records and pictures through years of Longhorn football history. It was a task continued by Doug Smith and Dave Saba in the 1980s and 1990s. All of them understood that the job of the sports information director was to preserve the past—and tell the story. Today, John Bianco and Scott McConnell have taken the profession to a new level, using modern technology to both recognize the past and communicate the present. They have never forgotten the roots.

Sansing, Evans, and Ramsey kept incredible photo files, which are now managed by Susan Allen Sigmon and her wonderful staff. Susan is a true artist with a camera, and her work accentuates the recent story of the Longhorns.

Thanks to Michael Urban and Mary Norris of The Globe Pequot Press, which has chosen to publish a series that highlights stories not just of Texas, but of college athletics in general.

Once again, Jenna McEachern has done wonders in editing, and my wife, Kim Scofield, has provided advice and love to a project that truly comes from the heart.

Thanks as well to DeLoss Dodds, Patti Ohlendorf, Butch

Worley, and Chris Plonsky at The University of Texas, bosses and friends who gave me the chance to do this. And my sincere appreciation to the many people who have encouraged me in my writing.

Finally, thanks to all of those who coached and played the game at Texas. Darrell Royal has been my friend and inspiration. Mack Brown has reignited the flame of excellence in Longhorn football. And hundreds of other coaches and players have touched us all.

This is their story.

Preface

In so many ways the small town of Winters, Texas, was a perfect place to grow up in the 1950s. We got our values from parents who had lived through depressions and wars. And there was a whole new world out there in an electronic revolution, which included creations such as television sets.

From our house across the street from the school, I could easily walk or ride my bike several blocks down Main Street to town, where the only stoplight spanned the corners between two drug stores, the bank, and a barbershop.

The local high school football field doubled as a rodeo arena in the summer. I was too little to play football or basketball, and I was an average tennis and baseball player and a worse golfer. I soon learned that my association with games would be to write about them, for my gift was to be able to tell the story. With a mother who was a writer and a dad who was a photographer, journalism was a natural path for me.

As kids, my brother Harvey and I heard the stories about how my mom had attended The University of Texas when she was just fourteen years old, and we knew my dad had played both freshman tennis and baseball under Longhorn legends Dr. Daniel Penick and Billy Disch.

We had even attended a reunion of Dad's old fraternity in the mid-1950s. But in my sophomore year in high school, in the fall of 1957, everything changed. Texas had hired an exciting young football coach named Darrell Royal. The black-and-white television brought pictures, and the radio brought us the play-by-play. And Royal, and the members of his teams, became my heroes. In the fall of 1960, I entered the university, and by the next year I was writing sports for the *Daily Texan*.

This book is a collection of a few of the many, many tales that make up the mosaic of Texas football. What I have tried to do is capture the moment, and the spirit, of the time.

Most of all, it is about people, because that is what sport is about. It is a reflection of life . . . of its accomplishments and its setbacks. And, finally, it is about the joy of the human spirit, which defines us all.

The Early Years

It was a manly sport, this football, and for almost twenty-five years, those "Yanks" at the likes of Harvard, Rutgers, Princeton, and Yale had played the game with a fervor that captured the headlines in the newspapers and magazines of the time. The University of Texas was a small college in Austin that was ten years old in 1893 and was going about the business of trying to establish itself as a "University of the First Class," the way the founders of the Republic—and later the state—had envisioned it fifty years before.

Through the mist, picture the way it was that November night when fifteen or so "wannabe" football players and a couple hundred fans gathered at the train station in Austin for a ride to Dallas. It was nearly midnight when the train crew of the International and Great Northern Railroad—its enormous engine straining to go—finally heard the conductor shout, "All aboard."

Thanksgiving morning, 1893, dawned a new day for that college in Austin, for those young men were destined for Fairgrounds Park in Dallas, where they would play the vaunted Dallas Football Club, the self-proclaimed Champions of Texas. Unbeaten for several years, and unscored on for a time as well, the Dallas club had heard a team had been formed at the state university down in Austin. The bruisers from Dallas issued a challenge for the upstarts to "come on up." The game was set for Thanksgiving Day in the hopes that it would draw a crowd in

The 1893 Texas team took an all-night train to Dallas for its first game.

Dallas, which was then a bustling city of nearly 40,000.

To understand the game you must first understand the rules, and it helps to know that what the game folks saw that day was considerably different than the game we know today. The first college game between Rutgers and Princeton had been played in 1869, as fifty students participated in what amounted to a group of guys pulling off their coats to engage in a primitive game of soccer.

By 1893 eighty-eight colleges had football teams, and the game had been scaled down to where eleven players were on each side while on the playing field, which was 110 yards long.

Writer-historian Lou Maysel, in his book *Here Come the Texas Longhorns*, further explained the game of the day.

> . . . (the) goalposts (were) at each end and there was no end zone area. The ball was put into play from scrimmage by the center shoveling the ball back to his quarterback, who always handed it off to another player. Only lateral passes were legal, which made the game primarily one of frontal power runs. End runs were occasionally tried, but defensive ends were always played extremely wide to avoid being outflanked. The necessity of making only five yards on three consecutive downs to get a new set of downs also dictated straight ahead football.
>
> Teams could station any number of players on the line and tight mass formations were used. Players behind the line could start forward before the center shoveled the ball back and momentum plays employing this practice were the vogue then. Often, teammates would push or pull the ball carrier forward for additional gain while the

defensive team tried to wrestle him down or carry him backward. Kicking was an integral part of the game then, as it is now, but the scoring was different from today's system. A field goal was worth five points, while a touchdown produced only four points. A successful goal-after-touchdown (free kick) counted two points, as did a safety.

The Texas team arrived in Dallas at 8:30 that morning and quickly showed the Dallas ruffians they meant business, too. "When we got there," recalled guard Billy Richardson, "we all bought big cigars and strutted down Main Street." The day quickly took on the bantering that would later become famous in Dallas as the Texas-Oklahoma weekend.

Fans of the Texas team began their own yell, which went like this:

> Hullabaloo, hullabaloo,
> 'Ray, 'ray, 'ray.
> Hoo-ray, hoo-ray.
> Varsity, varsity, U. T. A.

In his book Maysel recalls that a young newsboy listened to the yell and then responded in a loud voice:

> Hullabaloo, hoo-ray, hoo-ray,
> Austin ain't in it today, today.

But he would be proved wrong. "Varsity," as the team was known, took the field with determination on that mild November day.

How Texas Became the Longhorns

In the season of 1903, The University of Texas football team was generally referred to as "Varsity." The student newspaper, the *Texan* (which would later become the *Daily Texan*), was in its infancy. Under orders from his editor, a sportswriter named D. A. Frank began calling the team the "Texas Longhorns." The reasoning was that through constant usage, the name would stick. By 1906 it was in constant use, but it didn't become firmly established until 1913, when H. J. Lucher Stark, a wealthy former student manager, gave the squad a number of orange-and-white blankets emblazoned with "Texas Longhorns."

"When the teams came out for the game, a spectator who had never seen football before was first taken by the players' bushy hair, which gave them their only cranial protection," wrote Maysel. "Uniforms consisted of lightly-padded breeches and homemade canvas vests tightly laced over long-sleeved jerseys. Heavy stockings and shoes, some with homemade leather cleats nailed on, completed the battle gear of that day."

Wrote the *Dallas News*, "To a man who has never heard of Walter Camp and doesn't know a halfback from a tackle, the professional game of foot ball [sic] looks very much like an Indian wrestling match with a lot of running thrown in."

At Least He Didn't Fumble

Prior to their first game against Dallas in 1893, the young Texas team played a practice game that was basically an intrasquad game on a field just outside of Austin. But the game got off to a slow start. The action had just started when Al Jacks, an Austin baseball figure who was not a student but played on the second team, grasped the ball so tight it burst. The players and the 700 or so fans who had gathered to watch had to wait thirty minutes while a student rode into town on horseback and returned with a new ball.

Not in their wildest imagination could those young men of the late nineteenth century have envisioned where their game might lead. Even getting to Dallas wasn't an easy task in those days. Where today's football teams travel first class and stay in five-star hotels, the eager collegians of 1893 didn't have adequate funds to make the 200-mile trip to Dallas. A local clothing goods store, Harrell & Wilcox, loaned the team $100 to cover food and lodging. The ticket agent for the International and Great Northern Railroad, a fellow named Peter Lawless, supplied the round-trip tickets for the team.

There were only a couple of buildings on the campus of the young university. The town itself, Texas's capital Austin, had just 15,000 residents. University tuition was only $30, and that allowed a student to attend as long as was needed in his course of study. To get into school, a diploma from an approved high school was the only entrance requirement. Graduates of Sam Houston Normal (now Sam Houston State) and Texas Agricultural and Mechanical College were also accepted. You could earn a bachelor's degree in the arts, literature, science, civil engineering, and law, and a medical degree was available at the university's branch in Galveston.

It had taken nine hours to get there on the train, but when the big engine pulled into the station in Dallas, the city was awake and ready for a festive day. The grandstand on the Exposition Grounds of the State Fair was packed long before the scheduled 2:30 P.M. kickoff. It was almost balmy, particularly for a late November day, as the temperature reached the low seventies. But as 2,000 people watched—the biggest crowd ever to see a game in Dallas up to then—the day was about to really heat up.

Even though the Dallas team had a reputation as the giants of the gridiron, there actually wasn't much difference in the size of the young collegians and the seasoned city fellows. Both the Texas and Dallas teams supposedly averaged almost 162 pounds per man, and the backs for both teams weighed in at between 135 and 155 pounds.

The teams were full of colorful characters, but none more so than the workhorse of the Texas offense, a young cowboy from Ballinger, Texas, named Addison "Ad" Day. Not only was Day the main rusher for the team, he was the first kicker in school history. It was Day who would set the tone as the game began.

Texas took the opening kickoff of the game and drove down the field using power plays. When Day pounded the center of the line right at the Dallas goal and the ball popped free, team-mate James Morrison, a tackle, picked up the ball and ran in for the first score. When Ad Day kicked the ball through the goal posts for the two-point conversion, the young college kids had a 6–0 lead.

Dallas would never recover. Day scored another touchdown and kicked the ensuing goal, but by halftime, the Dallas Football Club had regrouped and cut the score to 12–10.

The forty-five-minute half was followed by a bicycle race at intermission, and the officials needed the time. There were no penalties in those days for "unsportsmanlike conduct." Players regularly argued openly with officials, so much so that referee Fred Shelley of the Austin Athletic Club got enough of Dallas's bickering and quit after the first half. His fellow official (there were only two), umpire Tom Lake of the Fort Worth football team, recruited one of his teammates to be the referee for the final stanza.

But when the second half started, there was Addison Day again, pounding his way and finally running 15 yards for a touch-down and kicking the goal for an 18–10 lead. With a minute remaining, Dallas scored again, but the touchdown and kicked goal only narrowed the score to 18–16. Under the modern table of points, that would have been a 21–20 Texas victory.

If the goal of the Dallas team was to intimidate the colle-gians, it didn't work. Texas played the full ninety minutes with only one player leaving for an injury. Dallas's reputation for roughness was answered by Texas.

Maysel, writing of the game in his book, recounted a con-versation with tackle Robert E. Lee Roy, who went on to be a dis-

Some Things Never Change

A lot of folks think that criticism of teams and coaches arrived with the advent of radio talk shows and the Internet. Not so. One of the most successful coaches in the early days of Longhorn football was Dave Allerdice, whose teams carved a 33-7 record over five seasons from 1911 through 1915. At the end of the 1915 season, Allerdice resigned. He confided to friends during that year that the season would be his last "because of the supercritical nature of the Texas fans."

trict judge in Fort Worth. "He did not name the team involved," wrote Maysel, "but from his references, it was clearly the Dallas gang."

"We went up against one team that had the reputation of being a killing team and before we went to the town to play them, our captain, Paul McLane, taught us a 'killing code' just in case," Maysel quoted Roy as saying. "The game had not been going long until the other side made a deliberate attempt to break the leg of one of our men. Then McLane gave us the 'killing code' and we put three of the other side out in less than ten minutes of play. The captain of the other side called for time and came across with the request we try to play the rest of the game without any rough stuff."

The upset victory so stunned Dallas that end Tom Monagan, who played the game with a broken finger suffered early in the fray, said afterwards, "Our name is pants [mud], and our glory has departed."

"With that," wrote Maysel, "he pulled on his overcoat, jerked his cap down over his eyes, wiped some blood off his face and started for home."

For the Texas team, the fun was just beginning. John Henry "Baby" Myers, the team heavyweight at 210 pounds, had handled the kickoff return duties, even though he was a center. He claimed he had just gotten the hang of the game when time ran out.

"Why are we quitting now?" he asked teammate Morrison. "It's nowhere near sundown."

Later that school year, in February 1894, the two teams would meet again. This time the game was in Austin, and the weather was bone-chilling cold. The Hyde Park area just north of the campus was just becoming a suburb, and it was the site of the new field where the game was played.

Despite the cold and a high admission price of 50 cents, 1,500 spectators came by horseback, streetcar, buggy, carriage, coach, and on foot, prompting the *Austin American–Statesman* to say they came "in everything but balloons." Fans built campfires around the edge of the roped-off arena to battle the cold and drizzle.

The determination of the dethroned challengers from Dallas wouldn't be enough. Texas had some dazzling plays, including a 50-yard touchdown run by Jim Morrison and a "criss-cross" play that also covered 50 yards for a score.

I'll Flip You

Paul Simmons was a fine runner and a slashing tackler, and he was one of the early stars of Texas football. But he had one other asset that made him different from all of the other players of his time. Simmons, you see, was a talented tumbler—today we'd call him a gymnast—and he used that unique ability as a running back.

The 1913 Texas team was going through growing pains in this new game of football. They had seen the advent of the forward pass and learned about eligibility rules. They were unbeaten at 6–0 when Kansas A&M came into Austin on a cold, drizzly day for the next to last game of the season.

Texas scored 20 points in the first quarter and went on to a 46–0 victory. Three Longhorn players, including Paul Simmons, scored two touchdowns. But the game's most spectacular play belonged to the 175-pound Simmons. On one of his runs, Simmons came down to the safety man and executed a diving somersault.

Historian Lou Maysel quotes Simmons's teammate, Alva Carlton, as saying, "It was the darndest thing you ever saw. He had it so well timed that often his back would hit on the tackler's back. He'd just turn over and keep on running. All the surprised safety tackled was air, while Simmons went on for a touchdown. It was quite a sight to see."

Simmons's effectiveness was finally limited in the 1913 Texas–Notre Dame game, when the Irish, who had been tipped off to his style, stopped him by standing up and catching him in mid-air. But that was just a bump in the road for Simmons, who in 1915 set the school record for touchdowns in a game at four, and though tied many times, it stood until Ricky Williams broke it with six in a game in 1998.

As in the opener, the game featured the violence of the time. Texas Billy Richardson was kicked in the head, and Myers, the big center, picked up the Dallas player who did it and pushed his face in the cold mud and then sat on him.

"Here's getting even for you, Billy," Maysel quoted Myers as saying, an action that almost caused an all-out brawl.

The team would celebrate a 16–0 victory, and Texas football was on its way.

Emerging from those early days of Texas football was perhaps the most interesting character in the university's young history, and he wasn't even a player. He dressed in a black suit, with a black Stetson hat, and he touched more football players—with his hands and with his heart—than any man in the first twenty years of Texas athletics.

Henry Reeves was a special kind of pioneer. He was born April 12, 1871, in West Harper, Tennessee. He was the son of freed slaves, a black man who set forth to make his mark in a new world of freedom.

No one knows when he came to Texas, but he was a fixture in athletics almost from the beginning. He carried a medicine bag, a towel, and a water bucket.

In fact, Henry Reeves became almost as well known as the football team itself. The cries of "Time out for Texas," and "Water, Henry," brought the familiar sight of his tall, dark figure quickly moving onto the field. There he would kneel beside a fallen warrior, or patch a cut, or soothe a sore muscle.

"Doc Henry" he was, and in the twenty-plus years from 1894 through 1915, he was a trainer, masseuse, and the closest thing to a doctor the fledgling football team ever knew.

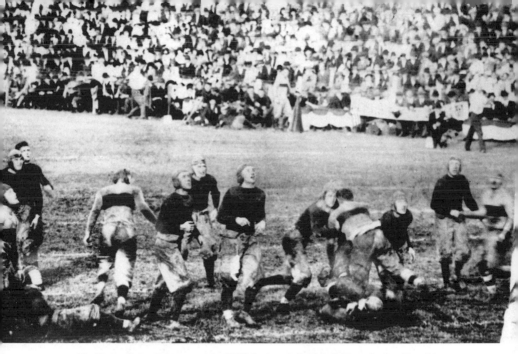

The Texas–Notre Dame game in 1913 featured an Irish field goal, as well as future legendary coach Knute Rockne, shown as a Notre Dame player, second from right.

In the publication the *Longhorn* of 1914, he was called "the most famous character connected with football in the University of Texas . . . He likes the game of football, and loves the boys that play it."

Once, a new athletic administrator tried to dismiss him, and the students rose up in protest. Henry Reeves stayed on. The *Cactus* yearbook listed the all-time teams of the early days, and one team was picked by coach Dave Allerdice. The other was called "Henry's team."

As the team boarded a train to go to College Station to play the Aggies in 1915, Doc Henry felt a numbness that all his self-taught medical knowledge couldn't cure. He went on to the game, but by halftime the stroke that would kill him had paralyzed the lanky trainer so that he could no longer run.

Henry Reeves lingered for two months after the stroke, and the entire student body took up a collection to pay his medical bills. The athletics council voted to award his widow a small pension.

When he died, the *Houston Post* gave him a special tribute. To put it into perspective, it is important to remember that in that day, a black man could not attend The University of Texas nor, for that matter, eat at the same table with the men he treated.

The news of his death will be heard with a sense of personal loss by every alumnus and former student of The University of Texas, whose connection with the institution lasted long enough for him to imbibe that spirit of association which a quarter century and more of existence has thrown around the graying walls of the college.

No figure is more intimately connected with the reminiscences of college life, none, with the exception of a few aging members of the faculty, associated with the University itself for so long a period of time.

In the hearts of Longhorn athletes and sympathizers, Doctor Henry can never be forgotten. A picture that will never fade is that of his long, rather ungainly figure flying across the football field with his coattails flapping in the breeze. In one hand he holds the precious pail of water, and in the other the little black valise whose contents have served as first aid to the injured, to many a stricken athlete, laid out on the field of play.

"Doc Henry" Reeves, shown here treating an unidentified Longhorn player.

Henry Reeves left the young university a message that it would take years to resolve. It was a message that the color of a man's skin made no difference in his mind, his skill, or his heart. All are given a chance to make of themselves what they choose.

The team's early success wouldn't end until the final game of 1894, when, after nine straight shutouts and ten straight victories, Texas would be upended by Missouri. As celebratory as things had been after victory, they were ignominious in defeat.

Texas had begun the year with a 38–0 defeat of Texas A&M in its first collegiate game ever and then took on what was expected to be a strong Tulane team in 1894. Tulane also was in its second season of football, and the folks in New Orleans accepted a huge guarantee of $400 to make the trip to Austin.

Texas won, 12–0, and Day not only pounded out yardage on the ground, he kicked the two extra goals in the game. In those days, the kicker was allowed a free kick following the touchdown. His only challenge was to put it between the goal posts . . . and not break the holder's hand.

A pounding of Arkansas, 54–0, and the San Antonio town team, 57–0, had set the stage for a dramatic season finale. Things did not go well. Three thousand fans came, only to see the Missouri Tigers jump to an early 12–0 lead and go on to a 28–0 victory. The fans left angry; some things haven't changed in all those years of Texas football.

The defeat was so stinging that some of the Texas players cut their long hair to hide their identity, and some left school and never played again. One of them was Ad Day, who went back to punching cattle. Years later, while living in Alberta, Canada, Ad recalled in a letter, "We were getting pretty swell-headed by the time Missouri came along and tore up our line like it wasn't there. I sneaked out of town that night and cut out my 'football course' at The University of Texas."

The glory run that had begun with young men meeting a challenge in Dallas ended with a strong reality check.

There would be an interesting theme to that season's end, however—a strand that would continue to weave itself through Texas football history. Before that season-ending game with Missouri, the manager of the Stanford team asked Texas to play them in Los Angeles. When Missouri won, the L. A. game was canceled.

Seven years later, in Pasadena, California, the town folks who held an annual parade celebration were looking for something to help finance their parade. And they thought they would try something with this game of football, which was gradually making its way across the country.

They called the parade the Tournament of Roses.

They called the game the Rose Bowl.

And one day, Texas would play there.

The Concrete Dream

It was like going through an old trunk hidden away in a dusty attic. The big steps leading to the entrance to historic Gregory Gymnasium had seen their travelers—people trekking up them for everything from a Louis Armstrong concert to fifty or so years of basketball memories.

But underneath the steps, hidden between a stockade-type wooden door on the south end and a barred open window on the north, was a storeroom full of relics of Texas athletics history. And that is where our story begins.

Eighty years ago, Texas students had dared to dream.

The idea of a concrete stadium to replace the wooden bleachers at old Clark Field actually had been stirred the year before, when athletics director L. Theo Bellmont held a meeting with thirty student leaders at the university cafeteria. That prompted a general meeting of the entire student body, and from there the idea went to the Board of Regents.

The cause was two-fold. First, it was to build a facility the likes of which had not been seen in this part of the country. And second, it was to honor the 198,293 Texans who served in what was then called The Great War—World War I. It was especially dedicated to the 5,280 Texans who died in that war, many of whom were recognized on the big plaque at the north end.

It would be named Texas Memorial Stadium, to honor all Texans, not just those who went to The University of Texas. It would be the students who would lead the effort. The first phase of the $500,000 subscription goal was the campus drive.

On a hillside east of Waller Creek between Twentieth and Twenty-Third Streets, on a thirteen-acre tract, the builders set the stakes. Dynamite blasted away the rock; horse-drawn equipment hauled the dirt away. A 27,000-seat stadium was their goal, and they vowed to finish it by Thanksgiving 1924.

Excavation began the first of April. Seven months later, on November 6, 1924, Texas played Baylor in the very first game, before a crowd of 13,500. Just as they had planned, the stadium would be dedicated a few weeks later, when a record crowd of 33,000, including fans in bleachers at the north and south ends,

Texas Memorial Stadium as it looked at the dedication day game between Texas and Texas A&M on Thanksgiving Day in 1924.

watched the Texas Longhorns beat Texas A&M by a score of 7–0.

The original construction included just the east and west stands, and though it has been remodeled several times, that core of the stadium remains. A north end, completing what was then a "horseshoe" was added in 1926. Extensions, supports, upper decks, and stadium suites have all been part of the metamorphosis. When construction of an east-side deck and stadium suites was planned in the mid-1990s, legendary coach Darrell Royal agreed to allow his name to be added to the stadium name. But it was only with the expressed stipulation that the name "Texas Memorial Stadium" would always remain as a tribute to those Texans who have served in all wars.

But stadiums, like universities, are not built of brick and mortar—they are about the people. And when it comes to war heroes, three powerful images of patriotism and Longhorn football intertwine.

The first, and still the most honored, was Louis Jordan. One of the most popular students at The University of Texas from 1911 through 1915 was a young man of German heritage from Fredericksburg, Texas, named L. J. "Louis" Jordan.

Jordan was like everybody's big brother. He was a round-faced blond who stood over 6 feet tall and weighed 205 pounds— that was big for the time. By timeless standards, he was exactly what you would want in a student athlete.

Jordan, in fact, was so gentle by nature he had to be coaxed to play football. But when he did, he became the greatest lineman, both offensively and defensively, of his era. He became the first Texas player to earn national recognition, earning Walter Camp second-team All-America honors in 1914. It is significant that this was a time when people in the East barely recognized that football was played west of the Mississippi.

Jordan made the electrical engineering honor roll every year, and he helped Texas teams post a 27–4 record during his four years, including a perfect 8–0 mark as a captain of the team his senior season of 1914.

Jordan's most famous moment as a Longhorn player came at the Oklahoma game that year. The Sooners' Hap Johnson ran the opening kickoff back 85 yards for a touchdown, and Oklahoma hopes soared. In those days, opposing fans openly bet with each other, and a lot of Oklahoma money went up at that moment. While the bets were coming, Jordan gathered the Texas team around him for the ensuing kickoff.

Clyde Littlefield, one of the Texas legends who was playing

The Audience Is Listening

Longhorn football has provided some groundbreaking moments in the broadcasting of live athletic events, and it all began with a game between Texas and Texas A&M in College Station in 1921. The game ended in a 0–0 tie, but history was made when two Aggie cadets transmitted a play-by-play with prearranged abbreviations over station 5XB in College Station to station 5XU in Austin. It was the first game account transmitted by wireless in the southwestern United States.

Thirteen years later, the Longhorns became part of the first network broadcast of Southwest Conference football. Interest in the Rice-Texas game in 1934 prompted the Humble Oil Company to put together three clear channel stations—KPRC in Houston, WOAI in San Antonio, and WFAA in Dallas. It was the beginning of the lengthy run of Humble's (later Exxon) sponsorship of what would become the Southwest Conference football network.

Texas notched another first in 1948, when WBAP-TV in Fort Worth televised live the Texas-Oklahoma game. In the 1953 Cotton Bowl game, the Longhorns played Tennessee in the first nationally televised New Year's Day game, a contest aired by NBC.

on the team, remembered the speech until the day he died. "He told us in no mincing words, with a few cuss words in German and some in English, 'Nobody leaves this field until we beat the hell out of them.'"

The Legend of Littlefield

The early era of Texas football produced no greater figure than Clyde Littlefield, who was one of UT's finest athletes and also an outstanding coach in both football and track in a career that spanned forty-eight years of Longhorn athletic history.

Littlefield won twelve letters in football, basketball, and track during his years at Texas (1912–16). The 6'1", 180-pounder was named to the Helms Foundation All-America basketball team and was the top scorer in the Southwest Conference's first season in both football and basketball.

In track he lost only one collegiate race and equaled the world's 120-yard high hurdles record. He also played briefly on the 1912 baseball team, but not enough to become the only four-sport letterman in school history.

Littlefield started his coaching career at Greenville, Texas, where his three football teams lost only one game. He joined the Texas staff as an assistant in football and head track coach in 1920. In the first spring in the newly finished Texas Memorial Stadium, Littlefield conceived the idea of a track and field carnival, and in 1925 the first running of the Texas Relays took place.

He became head football coach in 1927, and his teams won Southwest Conference titles in 1928 and 1930. When he gave up his football duties after the 1933 season, Littlefield's teams had carved a record of 44–18–6. He stayed on as track coach, and during his forty-one seasons until he retired in 1961, his teams won twenty-five Southwest Conference titles and finished second fourteen times.

Clyde Littlefield was a three-sport star as well as a football and track coach.

Let the record show that Texas scored 32 straight points, winning 32–7. Eleven men started the game, and the same eleven finished it, and an awful lot of Oklahoma betting money stayed in Texas.

Jordan lettered three years in track and four in football at Texas, and his athletic skill was superior to those players of his time.

They inducted Louis Jordan in the first class of the Longhorn Hall of Honor in 1957. He was one of only four men inducted and the only former athlete chosen. Sadly, he was not there to get the award.

As the years go by, fewer and fewer remember World War II, and almost none remember World War I. Only the history books and the Internet tell us of the Luneville Sector in France, where brave young men like Louis Jordan went to fight for that elusive dream of freedom and peace. Luneville was the "quiet sector" of France, where the French troops helped harden the young Americans for battle with Germany. It is ironic that a young man who was so proud of his German heritage would die from shrapnel from a German artillery shell.

News of the death of Louis Jordan, the first Texas officer killed in action, saddened the entire UT community. When they dedicated the new stadium in 1924 as Texas Memorial Stadium—in honor of the war veterans—the people of Fredericksburg erected a flagpole at the south end of the stadium where the Steinmark scoreboard stands today. It stood until 1971, when a new scoreboard was built. As a part of the stadium refurbishing at the turn of the twenty-first century, a new flagpole was erected, accompanied by the original plaque, and located in the southeast corner of the stadium.

At the same time Jordan was carving his Longhorn legend, another soldier was just beginning one of the most amazing careers of any Texas player. Kearic Lee Berry, known at Texas as "K. L.," was a letterman in 1912 and captain of the 1915 team.

Berry was a junior with a year remaining when he was called by the Texas National Guard to serve in France during World War I. He put in an extensive tour of duty and played football for an Army all-star team after the war. In 1924, the year Texas would dedicate the stadium to veterans, he returned to school to complete his degree. By that time, he was thirty-two, was married, and had three children. Despite a knee injury, which troubled him, he went on to earn All-Southwest Conference honors as a lineman, twelve years after he had begun his college career.

The legend of K. L. Berry was only beginning. He had entered the service as a private, but by 1942, he was a colonel in the U.S. Army in charge of the First Infantry Division of the Philippine Army on the island of Bataan. There, he would lead not only the First, but also the Third Division of the Philippine Army in the desperate battle that would eventually end in surrender to the Japanese. Berry would become one of the most decorated officers, earning the Distinguished Service Cross, before becoming the last U.S. officer to surrender his command on the island.

He was part of the infamous Bataan Death March, even carrying a comrade during the days-long forced march to POW camps. Moving from camp to camp, including transportation by unmarked Japanese ships (some of which were sunk by the U.S. Navy), Berry was incarcerated for forty months until the Russian army freed him and his fellow soldiers in September 1945 from a camp in Manchuria. He returned to Texas where he would attain the rank of Major General and Adjutant General of the Texas

National Guard. Like Jordan, he was inducted into one of the early classes of the Longhorn Hall of Honor, in 1959. He served as head of the Texas Guard until he retired in 1965, fifty years after serving as captain of the Texas Longhorn football team.

The most intriguing story of veterans who had Longhorn ties is that of Jack Chevigny, who served as Texas head coach from 1934 through 1936.

Webster defines odyssey as any long adventurous journey. Webster must have known about Jack Chevigny's fountain pen.

Gentleman Jack Chevigny was the new deal for Texas football when he became head coach. He was a suave, debonair man who had been a protégé at Notre Dame of the great Knute Rockne. In fact, had Rockne not died in a plane crash, most folks thought that his former star would have replaced him in the high-profile job of head coach of the Fighting Irish.

Chevigny came to Texas determined that he would make his mark against Notre Dame, and he did. In his first year, he took the Longhorns to South Bend and handed the Irish their first-ever loss in a home opener. The Longhorn team members were so impressed with the victory that they gave him a gold pen and pencil set engraved TO JACK CHEVIGNY, AN OLD NOTRE DAMER WHO BEAT NOTRE DAME.

Chevigny's early success at Texas didn't last, and by 1937, the Longhorns had made a coaching change. Chevigny went his way, and when World War II broke out, he became a Marine officer and was killed at Iwo Jima.

Walter Beach, who had served as the public relations man at The University of Texas in the 1930s, had borrowed the fountain pen many times when Chevigny was coach, but he never

The "Taste" of Victory

Ike Sewell was a good athlete at Texas. He played a little football; in fact, he was good enough to make All-Southwest Conference as a lineman. He also ran some track and got an education—and he began a love affair with The University of Texas.

When he left Texas, he went to work first for an airline company, then for a whiskey distributor, and then he was relocated to Chicago. For years he yearned for Texas, but his dream was to open a Mexican restaurant on the shores of Lake Michigan.

Trouble was, Mexican food didn't sell very well in Chicago. He was pretty frustrated with it all when a good friend who was in the restaurant business came back from Italy in World War II. He told Ike about an hors d'oeuvre he found in Rome—a small pie with cheese, meat, and tomato sauce.

On June 17, 1943, Ike Sewell and his partner opened a restaurant on Wabash Avenue in Chicago and called it Pizzeria Uno, the first restaurant in America—or anywhere else for that matter—to serve deep-dish pizza as a full meal.

It would become known as Chicago deep-dish pizza, and before Ike died in the 1990s, they had sold over fifteen million pizzas out of the little restaurant on Wabash and its sister down the street, Pizzeria Due.

Ike Sewell became an extremely wealthy man who was recognized as a Chicago business, sports, and charity leader. He supported the historical society and the Chicago Symphony Orchestra and a host of other charitable causes. In 1987 he was given the coveted Distinguished American Award by the National Football Foundation and College Football Hall of Fame.

His home and fortune were made in Chicago, but his heart remained in Texas. He never forgot his roots—that's why his company, with its restaurants and real estate holdings, is called the Saxet Corporation. That's S-A-X-E-T, as in Texas spelled backwards.

thought about it again until the commentator Bill Stern discovered a strange story.

As the closing act of World War II, the officers of the United States and Japan gathered on the battleship *Missouri* to sign the papers that would end the war. A U.S. officer noticed one of the Japanese officers was signing the papers with a shiny gold fountain pen. The officer asked to see the pen and read the inscription: TO JACK CHEVIGNY, AN OLD NOTRE DAMER WHO BEAT NOTRE DAME.

When the soldier saw that, he put the pen in his pocket and took it home to America. According to Stern, he found Chevigny's sister, who was living in Chicago. He gave her the pen that had been taken from the fallen warrior on the sands of Iwo Jima.

Frank Denius, a tremendous Longhorn fan who was a war hero as part of the D-Day invasion of Normandy during World War II, was a driving force in keeping "Memorial" in the mindset of everything involving the stadium. The North Gate, under the direction of Denius's Veterans' Committee, commemorates all of the foreign wars in which the United States has been involved.

Jordan, Berry, Chevigny, and all those who served as they did are important to us today because they represent what the game of football means. It is a challenge of the human spirit, and it is a contest played in mock war. They remind us that leadership and drive matter not only in a football game, but in life.

By the season of 2004, the legacy of the stadium had come full circle. Eighty years after it was first dedicated, it was the scene of a very special moment. Ahmard Hall, a sergeant in the Marine reserves, joined the Longhorn team as a walk-on football player. Hall had served in both Bosnia and Afghanistan and was attending The University of Texas under the G.I. Bill. As a tribute to the

Jack Chevigny brought the Longhorns their first big national win, beating his alma mater, Notre Dame, in 1934.

troops serving during the War on Terrorism, Hall led the eventual Rose Bowl champions onto the field at every game, carrying the American flag.

While the historic meaning of the stadium hasn't changed, there have been a few changes and additions that were completely necessary. When the most recent construction was undertaken, there was an odd requirement that had to be met before any other work could be done.

The modern facilities of any stadium required more restrooms, and the current planners were all for that. But first they had to spend $1.5 million to replace the sewer pipes. The basic stadium sewer system, built for the times in 1924, could handle only so much flow. You could add restrooms and toilets, but you couldn't count on the flush to go anywhere.

So there was that moment in the 1990s, when the sewer lines had been replaced, that athletics department employees were dispatched to the restrooms throughout the stadium, and on cue, they all flushed simultaneously to make sure the repairs were adequate.

That done, the builders went about the business of revamping the stadium to accommodate the needs of the twenty-first century.

In the new era Mack Brown and his Longhorns have done their part to add to the legacy. Since Brown came in 1998, the Longhorns are 38–3 and have won twenty-nine of their last thirty home games. Brown had urged Longhorn fans to wear orange, and they did. As the stadium has turned orange, it has turned into one of the toughest places for a visiting team to play. The only similar era was the "Royal run" in the late 1960s until 1976, when the Longhorns under coach Darrell Royal won a school-record forty-two straight at home.

We are taught that construction, whether it is of a football legacy or a building or a stadium, happens one brick at a time. And that was the irony of the storeroom under the old steps of Gregory Gym.

I had heard stories from my dad, who played baseball and tennis at Texas in the early 1920s, about that fund drive. He talked of how the students rallied and started the fire that eventually ignited the alumni and the state to build the stadium.

And there, in an old flat file cabinet, were the yellowed 3" x 5" cards labeled "student contributions." There was one girl who had made a pledge and donated to a blood drive to fulfill it. But when I got to the Ls, I felt like the kid in grandma's attic.

"W. E. Little," it read. And the amount was $10.

This story, however, is not about him, although I am sure that $10 in 1924 was a heckuva lot of money to a college kid playing two sports and trying to get an education. It is instead, about all of those whose vision and dedication made the stadium possible. Millions, probably closer to billions, of people have sat in seats on this hillside over a very long time.

And what matters here are the myriad things they celebrate. It is about college life, and all the remembrances of it. It is about men who fought, and those who died, so that we could be free. It is about a dad and mom and their sons and daughters who have spent an autumn afternoon or evening together.

In that space, it is not about winning or losing, although there are certainly lessons to be learned from both.

Maybe, after all, that is the message. It is the lesson we learn and the joy we share in the midst of a game, played in an arena because young people dared, and dare, to dream.

The Bible Era

The year was 1938, and the members of the Texas freshman football team were feeling pretty good about themselves after defeating the varsity in a regulation game. The country was trying to come out of a depression, and so was Texas Longhorn football.

The cavern had been deep. After a brief, shining moment when young coach Jack Chevigny's 1934 team defeated his alma mater,

Notre Dame, the program had fallen on hard times. After three seasons, ending with a 2–6–1 record in 1936, Chevigny was gone.

To replace him, Texas had taken a bold step. Paying him more than they paid the university president, the folks at the Austin campus hired Dana Xenaphon Bible. Bible had experienced great success at Texas A&M in the 1920s and was doing very well at Nebraska when he got the call to come to Texas.

Bible's hiring was huge news, but he inherited a program desperately in need of players. His 1937 team was 2–6–1, and in 1938 the Longhorns struggled to a 1–8–0 record.

Skeptics abounded. "Ali Bible and His Forty Sieves," joked opponents, but they would not laugh for long. Those who were about to be a part of the metamorphosis knew.

Noble Doss, one of the many stars who would turn the program around, remembers the moment well. "There were 125 of us who were part of that 1938 freshman class," Doss recalled. "We had all-staters from all over Texas. But times were hard, and we all needed money."

A scholarship meant $40 a month, but the players—the first to live in the new dorm—had to pay the university $30 a month for room and board. The university held out $7.50 a month to pay tuition, leaving the players $2.50 a month spending money.

"After we beat the varsity, we got together and chose a representative to go talk to Mr. Bible and tell him we needed more money," Doss said. With eager anticipation, the stars of the future waited for his reply.

In his unforgettable booming voice, Bible (who had a habit of smacking his lips before he spoke) sent back the message: "Tell the boys I will be glad to meet with them, one on one, each indi-

Hall of Fame coach Dana Bible is considered the founder of the Texas athletics tradition.

vidually, at any time." Not a single player dared do it.

Such was the respect held for Bible by the boys who became men in his time as coach. So much so that, even almost sixty years later, not a single man refers to him as "Coach" or "D. X." Without ever being told to do so, they all call him "Mr. Bible."

The remarkable career of D. X. Bible began after his graduation from his hometown college of Carson-Newman in Jefferson City, Tennessee. He was the son of a classics teacher, and he brought class and intellect to the growing game of football when he started his coaching career at Brandon Preparatory School in Shelbyville, Tennessee, in 1912. A year later, he was in college football, working at Mississippi College for two seasons. He took a job as freshman coach at Texas A&M in 1916 but wound up working "on loan" at LSU, where he took over as head coach midway through the season. He led the Tigers to a 3–0–2 record, and then he returned to Texas A&M as head coach for the 1917 season, where success was sudden and domination complete. His Aggie teams would go unbeaten and unscored-on in 1917 and 1919 (he served in the army in 1918), and his teams would win five Southwest Conference titles in eleven years there before he moved to Nebraska in 1929. His Cornhusker teams won six conference championships in eight years and had a 50–15–7 record—outscoring opponents 1,020 to 485.

Texas, meanwhile, floundered after the brief, bright love affair with young Chevigny dimmed. Jack Chevigny made $5,000 as head football coach at Texas, and most folks thought it impossible that Bible, who was earning $12,000 at Nebraska, could be enticed to come to Austin. It would take at least $15,000—almost twice what the university president was making—to get him. But

A Different Kind of "War Hymn"

In the closing days of World War II, the date of April 21, 1945, held special significance to all of the Texas A&M Aggie officers who had helped lead the Allied invasion into Italy. But a sly Longhorn in their midst turned the Aggie Muster into a Texas trick.

Bill Sansing was a young information officer for the forty-ninth bomber wing of the U.S. forces in Europe, and it was his assignment to help make the annual Aggie Muster—held on April 21 on the anniversary of the Battle of San Jacinto—a special occasion. So Sansing trained a dozen Italian young-sters—aged eight to eleven—to sing an American song in English.

The night of the party came, and the cherub-faced young-sters proudly strolled into the great hall. Four notes into the song—you guessed it, it was the "Eyes of Texas"—the generals were chasing Sansing out into the night.

It was a coup for Sansing, but his greatest work for The University of Texas was yet to come. D. X. Bible remembered Sansing as a young writer, and he had heard of his clever fun with the Longhorn rivals. When Sansing returned from the war, Bible hired him as the first university sports news direc-tor in this area of the country.

After establishing the office, Sansing would go on to immense business and public relations success, serving as a consultant to Jack Nicklaus and the Dallas Cowboys before he finally retired several years ago.

when Bible made a clandestine visit to Austin (he got off the train and walked to a waiting car to visit with Athletics Council chairman Dr. J. C. Dolley), the wheels were in motion.

Bible was hired, earning $7,500 as football coach and $7,500 as athletics director. The president's salary was raised to $17,500.

"It was Mr. Bible who laid the foundation of excellence for all sports at Texas," said Bill Sansing, who in 1946 was hired by Bible to become the school's first sports information director.

Bible built his program from the roots of Texas, creating "The Bible Plan." In a time when athletes were paid to play, Bible brought forth a plan, in his own words: "of simply selling our university to the athletes for its educational advantages, instead of paying the athletes their own prices to come play for athletic glory. When a boy is contacted and invited, he is told he will receive the benefits of being a member of the team only so long as he is eligible scholastically. But so long as he remains eligible, and in school, these benefits continue until graduation regardless of whether he is able to make the team, or is injured and cannot compete for the remainder of his college career."

He stood only 5'8", but he walked as a giant in a career that covered much of the first half of the twentieth century. He missed one season because he was in World War I, and his final years at Texas were affected by World War II. Still, he was the third-winningest coach in the history of the game—behind only Pop Warner and Amos Alonzo Stagg—when he quit coaching after the 1946 season.

He always wore a starched white dress shirt and a tie to the games, and he seldom moved from his seat on the team bench. But he had a flair for the dramatic. There were many defining moments in his Longhorn career. But the one Bible himself remembered the most came in 1939, when Texas trailed Arkansas, 13–7 with less than a minute to play.

Bible, who started the famed "12th Man" tradition at Texas A&M by calling in a player from the stands at halftime, sent a messenger to the Longhorn band, asking them to strike up "The Eyes of Texas." It was a moment the Cecil B. de Milles and Steven Spielbergs of the world live for. But had it not been for a young sophomore named Jack Crain, who had been part of that group too afraid to meet with Bible, Texas football might have a far different face today. In his various definitions of the word "renaissance," our friend Webster uses the words "rebirth" and "revival." That is what happened in 1939, when Jack Crain touched the ball in the final minute of play against Arkansas.

"Things had been down for so long," says Sansing, who watched the game as a student. "There was a loser mentality. We were losing again, 13–7, with a minute to play. No one could have expected what was about to happen."

Many in the so-so crowd of 17,000—who had come to see if the Longhorns could win their first conference opener since 1933—were headed to the exits. Only 30 seconds remained. In the huddle, quarterback Johnny Gill gathered his teammates and changed a play—and therefore the face of Texas football.

Gill directed Crain, the halfback, to switch positions with him. He told Crain to brush-block the end and drift out into the flat for a screen pass. Fullback R. B. Patrick took the ball, and he threw.

To that point, Texas had just 5 first downs and 78 yards of offense. Only an 82-yard quick kick return for a touchdown by Crain had put the Horns on the scoreboard.

Cowboy Jack Crain would become a Texas legend and would go on to serve in the Texas legislature, but nothing he would ever do would have an impact on something as much as his weaving run for 67 yards and a touchdown. Only seconds remained when he crossed the south goal line, tying the score at 13, and it took several minutes to clear the fans from the field so Crain could kick what turned out to be the game-winning extra point.

Years after his Hall of Fame coaching career was over, Bible recalled the significance of that moment. "That play and that victory changed our outlook—mine, the players', the student body's, and the ex-students'," said Bible. "Things had been going pretty badly up until that game. The way was still long, but we had tasted the fruits of victory and we were on our way."

The Longhorns finished 5–4 that year, posting their first winning season in five years, but the foundation was in place. Over the next seasons Bible would field some of the greatest teams in Texas and Southwest Conference history, and he would end his career at Texas as athletics director, a post from which he hired Darrell Royal as the Longhorns coach in December 1956.

Sansing, the wordsmith, said it best, and he didn't even have to look the word up in Webster. "It was the renaissance of Texas football," he said. "Before that, everything was down. After that, everything was on the way up." Bible's subsequent teams would be 8–2 (1940), 8–1–1 (1941), 9–2 (1942), 7–1–1 (1943), 5–4 (1944), 10–1 (1945), and 8–2 (1946).

Crain was an early one of many great stars who would play for Bible in his ten years as Texas coach. Another, Noble Doss himself, would become a legend, catching an over-the-shoulder

"It Couldn't Be Done"

From the time Texas Memorial Stadium opened in 1924 until 1956, the Longhorns never lost in Austin to their archrivals, the Texas A&M Aggies. The highlight of the games came in 1940, when the defending national champion Aggies were poised for a repeat title and a trip to the Rose Bowl.

Texas was a respectable 6–2 on the season entering the game, but few among the crowd of 45,000 that filed into the stadium that Thanksgiving Day gave UT much of a chance.

But the Longhorns stunned the Aggies with a touchdown in the first minute of play, set up by what would become known as "The Impossible Catch," an over-the-shoulder 32-yard reception by Noble Doss that carried to the Texas A&M 1 yard line.

The lone score would stand up, with Texas winning, 7–0. The spirited effort by his team, players would later say, was spurred by a poem entitled "It Couldn't Be Done" by Edgar A. Guest, which Bible read before the game. The poem begins as follows:

> Somebody said that it couldn't be done,
> But he with a chuckle replied
> That 'maybe it couldn't,' but he would be one
> Who wouldn't say so till he'd tried.

pass to lead to the only score in a 7–0 victory over defending national champion and archrival Texas A&M in 1940.

Crain and Pete Layden led the 1941 team to the pinnacle of college football. Before a late-season tie and a loss, many would rank this as the greatest team of its era, and perhaps the greatest in Texas football history. It was at the close of that season that one of the enduring traditions of Texas football was started.

The 1941 Texas team had been so impressive that it was featured on the cover of *Life* magazine. But when Baylor tied Texas, and TCU upset the Longhorns, hopes for a national championship began to look bleak. On Thanksgiving Day, Texas was about to make its annual trip to College Station to play the Aggies at Kyle Field. The Longhorns had never won at Kyle Field and had won only once in College Station.

It was then that a group of students sought advice from a fortune-teller named Madam Hipple. From her inner sanctum, they came away with one piece of advice: Burn red candles. Throughout the campus and the city, the flame ignited. Longhorn supporters bought every red candle in town and orders went out for more. On Thanksgiving Texas defeated Texas A&M, 23–0, and the Kyle Field jinx was broken.

The Legend of Red Candles lay dormant for twelve years. In 1953 with the Longhorns preparing to face a Baylor team that was unbeaten and battling for a national championship, Bill McReynolds, who was managing editor of the *Daily Texan*, broke out a call for red candles.

Again, the campus burned with frenzy. *Time* magazine called the candles "The most potent whammy in Texas tradition, and nothing to be lightly invoked. . . . "

A blocked extra point was the difference. Texas won, 21–20.

Efforts to revive the magic of the candles failed in the fifties, but with a team that won only one game in 1956, not much else helped either.

In 1963, as Texas drove for its first national championship ever, the red candles came out again for a Baylor game, and Texas won, 7–0.

During the 1980s, when environmentalists forced the halt of the Texas bonfire, Longhorn faithful turned to a midnight Hex Rally, where red candles were again featured. That tradition continues today; however, the story has evolved from a visit to a fortune-teller to an old Chinese legend of hex-breaking.

More than fifty years after giving her advice, Mrs. Augusta Hipple, who died shortly after the twenty-first century began, clarified her position. A strong voice answered the phone, and there was a slight chuckle as she began to tell the story.

"Our boys were really down, and they needed something to help them," she said. "I had just begun my practice when the young people came to see me. I told them that 'red means alert' and that they needed something to show the team they were behind them."

After Texas beat Baylor in 1953, Dougal Cameron, a Longhorn player at the time, put the candles in perspective. "Spirit," he said, "makes you play better than you can."

Mrs. Hipple, who insisted she never was a "madame," told fortunes until she was in her late eighties. "The most important person, from the cradle to the grave, is the person that is within you. That is healthy ego, not diseased conceit," she said. "The boys were struggling so; they only needed something to relax the child that is within us all."

The message of the red candles wasn't magic; it wasn't an ancient Chinese hex breaker. It was the simple truth that applies to whatever in life you choose to do. There is a "Force" out there when people band together in a common goal, and the strongest force of all is the bright, burning will that lives inside you.

History would remember the 1941 Texas team, but its dream of winning the national championship and playing in the Rose Bowl Game in Pasadena would be thwarted.

The Rose Bowl committee had wanted Texas to play Oregon State in its New Year's Day game, but the Longhorns had one final game remaining—ironically with Oregon. Fearing the outcome of that game, the committee asked Bible to cancel it, which he refused to do. The committee then invited Duke to play in their game.

Texas crushed Oregon, 71–7, on December 6, 1941. The next day, the world would change enormously, when the Japanese bombed the U.S. Naval fleet at Pearl Harbor. Bible's dynasty was about to take a new direction in a time of war. His final odyssey would include the greatest player of his era, a quarterback named Bobby Layne. Fact is, no one will ever be able to match the legend of Bobby Layne.

Bobby Layne could play with the best of them and party with the worst of them. He is in the College Football Hall of Fame and the NFL Hall of Fame, and if they had a hall of fame for guys who liked to have a good time, he'd be in that as well.

Perhaps his greatest moment came in the Texas-Missouri game that climaxed the 1945 season.

To understand all of it, it is important to understand the time. World War II was ending, and many young men who had gone to war were returning home. Bobby Layne was one of them.

Bobby Layne became the Longhorns' first All-America quarterback, then went on to a successful career in the NFL.

He had left Texas after his freshman season of 1944 and entered the Merchant Marine. As the war ended, he was discharged in the fall of 1945.

It was the middle of the season, and Rice had just beaten Texas in an upset 7–6 victory. In New Orleans, Bobby Layne was getting out of the service. A week later, Layne was back in uniform at Texas. The Longhorns quickly shook off the effects of the Rice loss, and with Layne playing fullback and tailback in the single wing formation, Texas swept through the remaining Southwest Conference games and earned a spot in the Cotton Bowl.

Missouri had lost three early games but had swept through what was then the Big Six conference. And so it was that the two schools were set to meet on January 1 in Dallas.

The tales of Bobby Layne at Texas would grow with time. But the fact is, most of them were true. As a quarterback, he would go on to play in four Pro Bowls in an eight-year window. As a college baseball pitcher, he was unbeaten in Southwest Conference play, going 28–0 in his four years.

His great friend Rooster Andrews loves to tell the story of a critical baseball series against Texas A&M in College Station. Texas needed a victory to keep its chances of a conference championship alive, but Layne had cut his foot rough-housing two nights before the game. He got the gash stitched, swore Andrews to secrecy, and enlisted his help.

Coach Bibb Falk always sat at one end of the bench, and Layne got Rooster to the other end. He paid Andrews to go buy a six-pack of beer. After each inning, he would sneak behind the bench, out of Falk's sight, and slug a bottle of beer.

"He was doing pretty good," Rooster recalled, "and as he

came to the seventh inning, he gave me some money to go buy some more beer." That day, Layne pitched a no-hitter.

The night before the Missouri football game in Dallas, Layne and Rooster put forth some Texas hospitality to some of the members of the Tigers team.

"Those Missouri guys were a good bunch," Layne recalled before his death in 1986. "We got to visiting at a Cotton Bowl luncheon on New Year's Eve, so I told Rooster to invite some of them over to our hotel that night for a little party. Nothing wild, mind you. Just some light refreshments and a good bull session. They headed back to their hotel well before curfew."

The next day, Bobby Layne accounted for every point in the Texas 40–27 victory. He ran for 3 touchdowns, caught a 50-yard pass for another, completed passes for the other 2, and kicked 4 extra points. He completed 11 of 12 passes for 158 yards. The only incompletion was a dropped pass by a receiver in the fourth quarter.

When the game was over, Missouri coach Chauncey Simpson went to the Texas bus to shake Layne's hand and told him, "I never saw a better job by anybody." Simpson later told the media, "It was too much Layne. Certainly we never ran into one like him before."

When he left Texas he owned every passing record in school history, and though time and different offenses have replaced most of them, one that still stands is the record for the winningest quarterback in Texas Longhorn history. Despite missing half of that 1945 season, he finished his career with a school record twenty-eight victories and only seven losses.

Bobby Layne played fifteen years in the NFL, and with his great friend, Doak Walker, he led Detroit to a pair of world championships.

The Little Indian

The inequity of it was striking, but then nobody ever said when the time comes, it would be fair. It was cold the day they buried Frank Medina. Bone cold. The ice was still on the trees as you looked out the church windows toward the lake, which was winning the battle against the freeze—as Austin lakes are apt to do.

But when you thought of Frank, you couldn't help but think of a warm training room, the kind of warm that would put a hitch in your first breath.

Frank Medina—an almost 5' Cherokee Indian—had served athletes from The University of Texas and around the world for over thirty years before a stroke ended his career in 1978.

It was D. X. Bible who brought Frank to Texas. Medina was born in Lincoln, Nebraska, somewhere between 1911 and 1915. He began his training career at Haskell Institute in Kansas and had served at Arizona State and St. Mary's of California before he came to Texas in 1945.

Working was his life. In addition to bringing the science of physical education into the training room, he added the personal touch of a friend and counselor to Longhorn athletes. He toured the world,

Bobby Layne died of a heart attack in 1986. He was only fifty-nine. Those who knew him would tell you there never was one like him, before or since.

Bible would end his career after Layne's junior season in 1946. Layne, teammate Hub Bechtol, and end Malcolm Kutner (who played from 1939 to 1941) all have joined Bible as members of the National College Football Hall of Fame.

serving as trainer for two U.S. Olympic teams and for the Turkish Olympic team in 1968. He took teams overseas twenty-two times and visited sixty-three nations of the world.

More than thirty of his pupils went on to become head trainers for collegiate and professional teams. He was a major contributor to the growth of sports medicine in general. He was an innovator who introduced physiotherapy and diathermy into the training room and was instrumental in organizing the off-season programs for athletes. He was a chief of the Cherokee Nation and was honored by every group he served.

Hundreds of athletes literally felt his touch. His classroom was the shining clean training room; it was the stadium field; it was the cliff at the baseball field; it was the gym floor; it was the stadium steps. The most significant tributes to Frank Medina always are personal—a product of the mind. Because that is where he challenged you. As good as he was with the tape and the liniment, the rehab and the exercise, the mind was where he did his best work. For the Longhorn football players with whom he worked, remembering Frank Medina is highly personal, because his relationship always came down to man to man.

His Texas teams won three Southwest Conference championships, all coming in his final five years as coach after he had turned the program around. His overall record at Texas was 63–31–3, taking his all-time record to 201–74–23.

Bible stayed on as athletics director after he retired and was the driving force behind the hiring of Darrell Royal as head football coach in 1956. With that, he stepped aside, remaining as a "consulting" athletics director until 1961, when at age seventy, he finally retired for good.

He actually wrote his own retirement story, noting that he was leaving, "having reached three score and ten (the slippers, pipe and rocking chair age)."

Bible continued, "In putting down names and events that I shall always cherish, the list is without end. I have a deep appreciation to all who have had a part in keeping me in the lineup—it takes so many to make a team."

But far beyond his immense success on the field, Bible's legacy is measured in the men that he coached.

"In 1975," Doss recalled, "we put together a reunion of the ten teams that had played for Mr. Bible. Thirty-five years after we all started getting together, 90 percent of all the players came back to pay tribute. They came from all over the United States, just for one night."

Bible, Sansing recalled, only allowed the affair with the stipulations that there would be no gifts and that he would not have to speak. But as the party neared its twilight, and Rooster Andrews was about to lead the "Eyes of Texas," Bible, who was in his eighties, rose to speak.

"I can't let this moment pass without reflecting," Bible said. "I am reminded tonight of the elderly woman who went to the priest and confessed that she had sinned by committing fornication. The priest looked at her, questioning her advanced years, and asked, 'Was this recently?' To which she replied, 'No, it was forty years ago. But I still like to talk about it.'"

"People hit the floor laughing," said Sansing. "They were slapping their knees and practically crying. It was vintage Mr. Bible."

Dana X. Bible died at age eighty-eight. He had earned induction into the Athletic Hall of Fame at Texas A&M and the Longhorn Hall of Honor, the Texas Sports Hall of Fame, and several national halls of fame, and he was given the coveted Amos Alonzo Stagg Award. He had served for twenty-seven years on the National Collegiate Football Rules committee and was a charter member of the American Football Coaches Association, as well as its president in 1934.

Bible's shadow on the Texas athletics landscape was best described by the historian Lou Maysel in his book *Here Come the Texas Longhorns*.

"Most of all," wrote Maysel, "Bible lifted the Longhorns from the league patsy to one of the respected football powers in the country. But perhaps Bible's most outstanding contribution at Texas was the order, stability, and prosperity he brought to the entire athletic program, which was in a state of disarray when he assumed the reins."

Bible's motto, which he borrowed from Teddy Roosevelt, was: "What we have a right to expect from a good American boy is a good American man."

More than sixty years from the day Bible first recruited him, Noble Doss could still see him in the "chalk room" with a pool cue–like pointer in his hand, going over and over every play the team would run and talking about life in the midst of teaching football—a little man with a commanding voice, who would never be forgotten by those whose lives he touched.

Darrell Royal: A Longhorn Icon

It had been almost thirty years since he had coached his last football game, but the moment was not lost on Darrell Royal as he moved through the crowd and down the ramp into the Rose Bowl.

DeLoss Dodds, the Texas athletics director, walked with him, and noticed the emotion in the eyes of the most famous figure in Longhorn football history.

He had just turned eighty, this man who had been associated with Longhorn football for almost half a century.

As the sea of orange swelled the pride within him, and as Longhorn fans and college football fans alike saluted him and his friend, Michigan's Bo Schembechler, in pregame ceremonies before the 2005 Rose Bowl game, Darrell Royal took time to remember.

As a boy he had come to California with his family, trying to make a living in the fields, fleeing the Dust Bowl days in his native Oklahoma. At the time, in the early 1940s, he was trying to get a coach to let him try out for the varsity football team and was dreaming of one day becoming a high-school football coach. It had been a long time since he had hitch-hiked back to Oklahoma to stay with his grandmother and work at the local Ford Motor Company dealership so he could go to high school and play football, the game that would become his destiny.

Years later, his classroom would be a stadium, and he would give his exams publicly, before thousands of people each Saturday in the fall. He taught not only the game, but he taught about life, and his students, as tributaries of a great river, carried his message far beyond the confines of the arena. Those who audited the class—the thousands in the stands and the millions watching on television—saw a man dedicated to his trade, to his responsibility, and to his players. When he arrived at Texas in December 1956, he was thirty-two years old—the youngest head coach in college football. He came to a program that had slipped to a 1–9 record, and he quickly set about restoring pride in the university, giving it unparalleled success for twenty seasons. More than 250 million— a quarter of a billion—people knew something about The University of Texas because they saw Royal's Longhorns on television.

Darrell Royal was treated to a lot of victory rides in his twenty-year career.

In 1962 he assumed the dual job of head football coach and athletics director. In his time as an administrator, he was directly responsible for the rise in excellence of all men's sports, and he was a guiding factor in the creation of one of the best women's programs in America.

Royal, who was named a professor and given tenure by the university during his great success in the early 1960s, was voted Coach of the Decade by ABC-TV for his work in that remarkable span between 1961 and 1970. In that time Texas won three national championships and six Southwest Conference championships, went to eight bowl games (winning six of them), and finished in the nation's top five seven times. When he quit coaching after the 1976 season, Royal was a young fifty-two years old. In twenty years his teams had won 167 games, 11 league championships, played in 16 bowl games, and claimed 3 national championships.

He stayed on as athletics director through the fall of 1979, helping to lay the foundation for stricter NCAA guidelines on recruiting and admission standards for student athletes. His career was highlighted by efforts to maintain high standards of integrity and honesty in the workplace of college athletics.

In 1980 he became a special adviser to the UT president on athletic matters, and he served full-time in that capacity until he retired and was retained on a part-time basis in 1990.

He was an innovator on and off the field. In the game he was responsible for creating two of the most potent offenses in football—the "flip-flop" Winged T formation of 1961 and the famed Wishbone that appeared in 1968—launching the Longhorns on a thirty-game winning streak that ranks as one of the longest in NCAA history.

The "Brain Coach"

When Darrell Royal was hired as the Texas football coach in December 1956, the administration offered to allow him to hire a person as a "recruiting coordinator." Royal surveyed the situation for the Longhorns, who had gone 1–9 in 1956, and determined that recruiting was not the most pressing problem.

"It looks to me like you are getting plenty of players," he told them. "It looks to me like our problem is keeping them in school."

So Royal went out and hired a high-school principal named Lan Hewlett to assist his players with their academics. Hewlett thus became the nation's first-ever academic counselor for athletics at a university, and he was fondly referred to as the "brain coach." In 2004–05, the university budgeted more than $2 million for student services, a large chunk of which is dedicated to academic support.

Off the field he created a position for the nation's first academic counselor for athletes. Royal stressed the importance of the college degree, creating a unique T ring, which he personally gave to lettermen who earned their degrees. Of the forty-eight lettermen on his 1963 national championship team, forty-five graduated.

As athletics director, he served on several NCAA committees, including the Television Liaison Committee, which dealt with national and regional televising of college football. In the early

The "T" Ring

In his first season at Texas in 1957, Darrell Royal created a unique award to recognize his student athletes. Royal designed a gold ring with an orange stone capped with a white T. He presented the ring as a personal gift to any Longhorn football player who lettered and achieved his degree.

In time, the athletics department took over the purchase of the rings, and the tradition was expanded to letter winners in other sports. In football, however, the tradition of the coach awarding the ring continues almost fifty years after Royal came up with the idea.

1970s when Title IX helped bring about the creation of women's athletics programs nationally, Royal helped craft Texas's plan to finance its program in a way that allowed complete funding without diluting the men's program.

But his service would go far beyond the university. He served on the Board of Directors for Stillman College, a small predominantly black institution in Alabama, and he parlayed his love of country music and golf into numerous fund-raising events that produced millions of dollars for underprivileged youngsters.

His honors are legion, from membership in the Longhorn Hall of Honor and the National College Football Hall of Fame to receiving the coveted Horatio Alger Award.

Raised in the days of the Great Depression in Hollis, Oklahoma, Royal played his college ball at the University of Oklahoma. He served in the Army Air Corps from 1943 to 1946 during World War II and entered the coaching profession in the early 1950s. He served as head coach at Edmonton, Canada, in the Canadian League, at Mississippi State, and at Washington before coming to Texas.

Royal always believed in Plato's theory that there were four kinds of people:

> Those who do not know, and do not know that they do not know;
> Those who know, but do not know that they know;
> Those who do not know, and know that they do not know; and
> Those who know, and know that they know.

And Darrell Royal knew.

. . .

The hour was late, and Darrell Royal was sleepless in Seattle long before they made a movie about it. As one of the young lions of college football, he did dare to dream, but even in his greatest fantasy, becoming the head football coach at The University of Texas was a stretch.

Royal was young, and as a college head coach he had had two 6–4 years at Mississippi State and one 5–5 season with Washington.

The Texas football job was one of the nation's plums. Publicity around the job search had mentioned such high-profile names as former Notre Dame coach Frank Leahy, Bobby Dodd of Georgia Tech, Duffy Daugherty of Michigan State, and Murray Warmath of Minnesota.

"I had kind of daydreamed about the opportunity of coming to Texas, and Edith and I had talked about it a lot," Royal once told historian Lou Maysel. "It's funny how it happened. I was looking for the call, yet at the same time I knew there was not much basis to be called."

But when the phone rang late that night and the strong voice on the other end of the line said, "This is D. X. Bible of The University of Texas," Royal put his hand over the phone, turned to his wife and said, "This is it, Edith. It's The University of Texas calling."

Everywhere Bible turned in his search for a coach, Royal's name surfaced with glowing recommendations, and when he came for the interview, he left with the job. His charm was obvious, and his winning ways instantaneous.

He came to the Austin campus with a folksy sense of humor that produced a phenomenon called "Royalisms" and a style of football that produced solid success.

Texas went from a 1–9 season in 1956 to a 6–3–1 regular season in 1957—and with it a trip to the Sugar Bowl. Royal's Longhorns were off on the first of sixteen bowl trips they would make over the next twenty years. In twenty-three years as a head coach, he never had a losing season.

In southwestern Oklahoma, Royal chopped cotton for 10 cents an hour as a kid during the Great Depression and began his life in football as a high-school star in the early 1940s. He was an All-America quarterback at the University of Oklahoma, and more than half a century later, he is still OU's all-time intercep-

T for Texas

One of the more significant figures in Texas athletics in the second part of the twentieth century was James Carroll "T" Jones. Jones quarterbacked the Longhorns in 1950–52 and was part of a Longhorn backfield that set a remarkable record with each of the four players earning All-Southwest Conference honors.

He led tenth-ranked Texas to a 16–0 victory over eighth-ranked Tennessee in the 1953 Cotton Bowl game and then joined the Longhorn coaching staff. When Darrell Royal took the head coaching job in December 1956, Jones was one of a couple of coaches whom Royal retained.

He remained on the staff through the 1962 season, when he left to enter private business. He returned to athletics in January 1980, when he became assistant athletics director at Texas. In 1985 he took the athletics directorship at Texas Tech University. He retired in 1993 and moved to the Horseshoe Bay retirement community near Austin, where he reconnected with UT athletics as a member of the Longhorn Hall of Honor Vintage Committee.

tion leader with seventeen. In his time at Texas, the Sooners would make several overtures to try to get him to come home to coach, but he never left.

Royal became the media's dream, always turning a phrase in a unique way. He coined sayings that became part of Americana, and they would be repeated again and again.

"Luck," he once said, "is when preparation meets opportunity."

Thirty years later, television personality Oprah Winfrey used the same quote.

Perhaps his most famous saying came when he was asked if he was planning any changes before a particular game.

"We're like the girl at the school party," he said, "we're gonna dance with who brung us."

Sometimes, some folks just didn't take it right. When he was forced to use a backup punter named Kim Gaynor because of an injury to his star Ernie Koy, Royal recalled the fellow who was being chided because his date wasn't particularly good-looking.

"Ole ugly is better than ole nuthin,'" Royal said.

And he spent the next day apologizing to Gaynor's family, some of whom took offense. From that time on, Gaynor was known around the media as "pretty ole Kim."

But Royal was far more than folksy sayings. The competitor in Royal seethed at losing. After his first Texas team lost to Ole Miss, 39–7, Royal gave away the bowl watch presented to him as a memento of the bowl game. The best way to combat hating to lose is to win, and Royal did that as well as anybody in the game. In his twenty years as the Texas coach, his teams won more Southwest Conference games (109) and more games (167) than any team in league history. His record of 167–45–5 was the best mark in the nation over the period from 1957 through 1976. His teams finished in the top ten nationally eleven times, and he coached seventy-seven all-SWC players and twenty-six all-Americans.

But as important as the wins were, it would be the honesty and integrity of Royal that would be remembered. With values etched by the winds and the dust, Royal came from a time and a place

Going for Two

The Texas-Oklahoma game in Dallas has always been a series of streaks, and it was a significant streak that the Longhorns had to challenge when they met the Sooners on October 11, 1958. The Longhorns, who were 13-point underdogs, had lost six straight games and nine of the last ten.

Darrell Royal, a former Sooner great, was in his second year as the Longhorn coach, and Royal had been an opponent of a new rule that came into effect that season in college football. The rule allowed a team to run a play from scrimmage after a touchdown and earn two points if successful. Prior to that, a point after touchdown, scored either by kick or a play from scrimmage, netted only one point.

So it was a surprise to everybody in the Cotton Bowl stadium when Texas, after scoring the first touchdown of the game, converted a two-point conversion for an 8–0 lead. The play would prove pivotal in the game, when Texas scored a touchdown with 3:10 remaining in the game and quarterback Bobby Lackey kicked the extra point for a 15–14 Longhorn lead.

When Texas went on to victory, it marked the first time in the NCAA that the two-point conversion play had decided a game. And it went in favor of a guy who opposed it in the first place. Royal then went on a streak of his own against his former school, as the Longhorns won eight straight and twelve of the next thirteen games in the series.

where sometimes all a man had was his will and his integrity. The benchmark of his career was the universal understanding that he ran a program where cheating would not be tolerated.

"I have a pretty strict code as far as athletics is concerned," he once said. "If you are playing under the real rules of golf, for instance, there is something weak in a person who moves his ball from behind a tree . . . who nudges his ball or mis-marks his ball.

"Adherence to the rules, sportsmanship, and ethics . . . those are the things we have to stand for. Athletics is a whole lot like life. You will always be tempted to 'cut across.' If you do that in college athletics, you are doing it with those who are the future citizens who will be leading our cities, our states, and our country. You are sending them the wrong message."

Royal and his dashing young staff—including defensive genius Mike Campbell, who would coach with him throughout his Texas tenure—flashed on the Texas football scene like a shiny new pocket watch. His first team defeated Bear Bryant's team led by Heisman Trophy winner John David Crow, 9–7. By 1959 he was competing for national honors, losing only to TCU in the ice in Austin, 14–9, and to national power Syracuse in the Cotton Bowl. The 1959 league championship was the first for Texas since 1953.

Two years later Royal would put Texas on the threshold of history. The 1961 Longhorns, featuring a running game that was as swift as it was powerful, rolled to number one in the national ranking before a 6–0 upset by TCU sidetracked them. But the 12–7 victory over highly regarded Ole Miss in the Cotton Bowl was Royal's first bowl victory, and it set the stage for a run that would include a 9–1–1 season in 1962 and the school's first-ever national championship in 1963. From the start of the 1961 season through mid-1965, Royal's Longhorns were an incredible 44–3–1.

Timing was everything for Darrell Royal. His 1967 recruiting class—dubbed "the Worster Crowd" because of the notoriety and prowess of fullback Steve Worster—was the nation's best. By the time they were sophomores in 1968, Royal had installed the Wishbone offense and was off on the thirty-game winning streak. As Royal's stature was growing, so was live sports television. The handsome Oklahoman with the winsome smile and the quick wit was an instant hit, and his teams appeared on television more than any other in the nation.

Conference championships in 1968, 1969, 1970, 1971, 1972, and 1973 were a record, as were six straight Cotton Bowl appearances.

But while he was teaching football, he was also teaching about life. With all his All-Americans and even a guy who would win the Heisman Trophy, Royal had no player more famous or more valuable than James Street, who quarterbacked the national championship team of 1969 and was never beaten in twenty starts as the Texas signal caller.

"The more removed I am from my days as a player, the more I appreciate what he did for me," Street said. "He had a way about him. He taught us how to live life with class . . . things like polishing your shoes and cleaning your fingernails were as important to him as the game of football. He didn't just teach you something, he gave you something. He put the lesson out there, and it was up to you to accept it. If you didn't get it, it was your own fault."

The lessons of life included a stroll back to the basics, and for Royal, life at times was tragic. It helped shape a compassion in him. Denne Freeman, a regional sports editor for the Associated Press and a good friend of Royal, always felt that Royal's zeal for coaching dimmed some with the death of his daughter, Marian, in an automobile accident in the spring of 1973.

"It definitely had that effect," Royal said quietly. "There is no question about that. It took away some of the sharp, aggressive edge. I wasn't quite as demanding after that. It didn't matter as much."

Several years later, the Royals lost another child when their son David died in a motorcycle accident. In times of tragedy for others, Royal is often the first to respond.

"You develop more compassion for others," he said. "It is something I can definitely relate to. All of us have lost members of our families, but there is nothing quite like losing a child. We always think we'll die before our children, but it doesn't work that way in all cases."

Once asked by a subordinate about the key characteristic of a person, Royal replied, "I have always thought the mark of a man is how he treats people who can never do anything for him."

That is why people loved Royal. Regardless of who you were, he made you feel special.

Perhaps the richest irony of the Royal career at Texas comes from the fact that in his early days, he was afraid of public speaking. A friend helped him by giving him a poem to learn, and when he had mastered the poem, he had conquered the fear. But the poem told a story that would best capture what Royal was all about.

"It's about the old guy who came to a chasm and crossed the chasm in the twilight of the evening and stopped, when he was safe on the other side, to build a bridge over where he had been.

"Some of the passersby saw the old man building the bridge and asked him why he built it. He was already across the chasm; why would he stop and build the bridge? He replied that a young person might follow along sometime, and they'd need that bridge to cross the chasm.

"It's a heckuva story . . . it tells a beautiful story, and I would wind up a lot of my talks with that . . . about the youth and what a great commodity they were and what a great asset they were. It wasn't oil, and it wasn't money that were our greatest assets. It was our young people. And we all should be trying to build a bridge for them," Royal said.

The poem read:

> An old man, traveling a lone highway,
> Came at the evening, cold and gray,
> To a chasm deep and wide.
> The old man crossed in the twilight dim,
> For the sullen stream held no fears for him,
> But he turned when he reached the other side,
> And built a bridge to span the tide.
> "Old man," cried a fellow pilgrim near,
> "You are wasting your strength with building here,
> Your journey will end with the ending day,
> And you never again will pass this way.
> You have crossed the chasm deep and wide,
> Why build you a bridge at eventide?"
> And the builder raised his old gray head:
> "Good friend, on the path I have come," he said,
> "There followeth after me today

A youth whose feet will pass this way.
This stream, which has been as naught to me,
To that fair-haired boy may a pitfall be;
He, too, must cross in the twilight dim—
Good friend, I am building this bridge for him."

"The Bridge Builder"
—Will Allen Dromgoole

In a tribute video to Royal shown at a celebration in 1996 announcing that his name would be added to the official name of the stadium on the UT campus, making it Darrell K. Royal–Texas Memorial Stadium, the words "Orange Towers *earned with effort* were all lessons in the stream" appeared. The author thought about changing them, but the young singer, a talented UT student named Emilie Williams, protested. The Orange Towers—symbols of victories—were, in fact, earned with effort, and there were lessons that were learned, she said.

"Exactly," said James Street. "It was all about effort. Whether it dealt with your personal life, or a game. He taught us that nothing comes easy."

At age fifty-two, following the 1976 season, Royal quit coaching.

"The downside of coaching was getting to me more and more, and the upside of it wasn't nearly as pleasing because all I was doing was trying to maintain a position. I had lost the really big thrill of winning, and the negative side of it was bothering me more and more. I knew the balance was such that it was time for me to quit. My time was at a rather young age. I still had plenty of energy and plenty of desire to coach, but I got to where I

Darrell Royal, whose name was added to Texas Memorial Stadium in 1996.
Susan Sigmon

couldn't stand losing, and I wasn't getting that much pleasure out of winning."

In the mid-1980s, Texas football hit a valley. The Longhorns, who had dominated the 1960s and were a presence in college football through the 1970s and early 1980s, disappeared from the national landscape. When the Texas administration decided to make their third coaching change in eleven years after the 1997 season, Royal was asked to serve in the selection process.

It was there that he became reacquainted with Mack Brown, the head coach at North Carolina and a person whom Royal had advised when Brown was head coach and athletics director at Tulane in 1985. While other candidates were mentioned prominently, Royal was part of a group that met with Brown and his wife, Sally, in Atlanta.

The bond was immediate, and it was strong. Brown became Royal's choice, which was certainly a helpful boost in his getting the job.

Brown reached out to Royal and his wife, Edith, in a very special way, and once again, he was embraced as a part of the Longhorn football family. Royal's pride in Brown's success, and his relationship with the young players on the Texas team, has energized the octogenarian. He's a regular at practice and was an honorary captain for the team that beat Michigan in the 2005 Rose Bowl.

There was a popular country song that once paid tribute to the legendary Bob Wills with the line, " . . . don't matter who's in Austin, Bob Wills is still the king."

As he turned eighty in 2004, so it was with Darrell Royal. When he walked into a room—almost thirty years removed from the game and nearly fifty from the day he first stepped on the Texas campus—heads would turn.

He has always had a presence about him, a presence of greatness achieved, of respect earned, and of a time and a place in college football that would never come again.

A Safe Place

It was battleship gray, the door to the old press-box elevator in the west side of Memorial Stadium, and fewer than five of us had keys to the solid padlock that guarded the door.

The elevator was hand-operated, and it stopped at the ground floor and at two of the three levels of the long concrete structure that sat atop the single-level stadium. The only entrance, other than the elevator, was a single door at the north end, which exited into the top row of the stands filled with wooden seats.

Except on game days, the door was barred from the inside.

On game days, the stadium buzzed with excitement. But if you had a key on a moonlit night and you wanted a place to show your date the stars and the lights of the city, you could ride that elevator up and no one, not Darrell Royal or God Almighty—and no one was sure they weren't the same—could make it come down.

In other words, in the autumn of 1963, it seemed the safest place on earth.

That press box and the Tower were the tallest buildings on campus. There was no Jester Center, no LBJ Library. The Moonlight Tower, which stood on the northeast corner of the stadium, cast a glow over the quirky baseball field across the street to the north and over the wooden roof of the tennis courts that were located on the northwest corner of the stadium.

And on the field below, with a black cinder track surrounding it, a dream came true that fall, that fateful fall of 1963, when all of our lives would change, and nothing would ever seem safe again.

Texas's quest for a national championship in college football had followed a star-crossed path. For years it seemed that the Longhorns and The University of Texas were riding on a great merry-go-round, and each time they reached for the gold ring, it somehow eluded them.

A couple of their Southwest Conference brethren—TCU in 1938 and Texas A&M in 1939—had earned the honor in the years since the Associated Press first began its poll in 1936. A loss to the Longhorns in 1940 even knocked the Aggies out of a second title.

The 1941 team, which was featured on the cover of *Life* magazine as the best team in college football, had fallen from contention with a late season tie and a loss.

Texas would produce top ten rankings four times in the eight-year period from 1945 through 1952, but it wasn't until Darrell Royal's third team finished ranked number four in 1959 that UT returned to the national landscape.

All that appeared to change in 1961. Royal's first SWC championship club was a powerhouse. With an innovative offense called the "flip-flop" because the offensive line and wingback would flip sides so as to simplify and maximize running plays, Texas steamrolled its opponents.

In a day of single-platoon football, Royal effectively used three different teams, and most folks thought his third-team backfield could play for anybody. The starting backfield featured All-America running back James Saxton, and Texas averaged over 30 points a game and yielded a scant 59 points to its competition during the entire regular season.

On November 4 the Longhorns shut out SMU in Dallas, and the results of the weekend left Texas ranked number one for the first time in twenty years. Two weeks later, however, the carousel of dreams would turn into a nightmare. In a stunning 6–0 shutout in Austin, a TCU team that would finish 2–4–1 in league play and 3–5–2 overall ended the quest. Texas would go on to win the first of Royal's eleven Southwest Conference titles and would beat Ole Miss in the Cotton Bowl. The 10–1 finish, the school's best since 1947, netted a number three national ranking.

Wished He Hadn't Said That

Oklahoma running back Joe Don Looney was the star of the 1963 Sooner team which was ranked number one in the country heading into its annual match with Texas in the Cotton Bowl in Dallas.

The Longhorns, ranked second in the country, had an outstanding defense, led by All-America tackle Scott Appleton, known as one of the toughest players in Longhorn history.

In a pregame interview during the week leading up to the game, Looney was quoted as saying "Appleton's tough, but he ain't met the Big Red yet."

It was a fatal mistake. Looney was tackled on the first play of the game for a 5-yard loss, and Appleton earned National Lineman of the Week honors as he made 18 tackles and recovered a fumble in the 28–7 Longhorn victory.

Said Looney after the game, "We were just too cocky."

The Monday following the game, Sooner coach Bud Wilkinson dismissed Looney from the team for disciplinary reasons, which did not include his pregame observations.

Texas was right back in the hunt in 1962. Despite the tragic death of a player due to heat exhaustion on the first day of fall practice, the Longhorns opened with five straight victories. They were never ranked lower than number three, and by the Arkansas game on October 20, they had moved to number one. In one of the most dramatic games ever in the stadium in Austin, the Horns drove 80 yards to score the game's only touchdown with 36 seconds remaining in a 7–3 victory over the number-seven-ranked Razorbacks. A defining goal-line stand, led by linebackers Pat Culpepper and Johnny Treadwell, had caused a fumble that Texas recovered midway through the third quarter.

A week later, everything would change.

It was an unreal feeling that night when Rice played Texas in Houston. There was a murmur in the crowd before the game, and the whispers were not about football. The humidity seemed to hang, as it can in Houston, and it almost seems there is a ghostly mist that hangs even now as the memory returns.

On the football field Texas was number one. The Longhorns had made sure of that with that 7–3 comeback win over Arkansas the week before.

But there was an eerie reality that night in Rice Stadium, as 70,000 people stood, their hearts pounding a rhythm, and their voices raised in a powerful singing of the national anthem.

Those who were there will tell you that until perhaps the patriotic swell that accompanied the events of 9/11 and the War in Iraq, they had never—before or since—heard the national anthem sung so proudly and defiantly.

Since Tommy Ford plowed over for that winning touchdown in the Arkansas game, football euphoria had reigned in Austin. Two days later, the real showdown came.

Early in October, when Texas was busy winning football games, the Soviet Union, under Nikita Kruschev, had moved 20,000 crack battle troops, forty intermediate ballistic missiles, and forty bombers capable of carrying nuclear warheads into Cuba, less than 90 miles from Florida.

On Monday, President Kennedy ordered a blockade of Cuba, and by the time Rice played Texas, the world had edged closer and closer to World War III.

Historians will say that it probably was—at least to our knowledge—the closest the world has come to nuclear war.

Four hundred thousand U.S. troops were on maximum alert. Weapons of war were loaded aboard ships and planes. Somehow, a football game that risked a number one ranking didn't seem important.

What was important, however, was a nation's pride. That is why they sang.

The game itself might as well have been played in the Twilight Zone. Rice Stadium had always been a tough place for Texas to play before the recent domination, but that year was beyond comprehension.

No one gave the Owls much chance, but as would happen often with the Owls' venerable coach Jess Neely, he had whipped "his boys" to a fever pitch to play Texas. The Longhorns never were able to get back up after the incredible "high" from the win over Arkansas. Texas trailed early, 7–0, but scored twice to make it 14–7.

Rice tied it, 14–14, and on a night when nobody appeared to want to be there, that's the way it ended. Texas would go on to an unbeaten regular season and the nation's number four final ranking. Rice would finish the year at 2–6–2, but the tie kept the Longhorns from a national title.

The game was only a brief distraction from the fear of the

greater conflict, a conflict that threatened life as we knew it. But on Sunday—the next day—the Good Guys won.

The Soviet Union relented and began removing its troops and dismantling the missiles. President Kennedy gave the order for the U.S. armed forces to stand down. The danger of the missiles of October was over.

That, however, was only a harbinger of the mixture of fate that would manifest itself in the lives of the young men of Texas football in the early 1960s.

What 1961 and 1962 had done was create a strong winning tradition, and with an all-star cast, Royal and his staff were ready for 1963. The Horns began the season ranked number five. They moved to number four the second week, number three the third week, and by the fourth week of the season, they were number two as they headed for Dallas and the annual meeting with Oklahoma.

Since Royal's first season of 1957, the Longhorns had not lost to the Sooners, but the national voters, the writers and the coaches had installed number-one-ranked Oklahoma as a favorite. Joe Don Looney, the Sooners star running back, had even challenged the biggest name on the Texas defense, Outland Trophy winner Scott Appleton, by saying, "Appleton's tough, but he ain't met the Big Red yet." Neither, he would find, had he met Appleton.

The annual showdown in Dallas was the biggest game, but it came on a weekend of irony. The Friday night before UT and OU met, SMU knocked off the power of the East, Navy, and Heisman Trophy winner Roger Staubach, in the Cotton Bowl Stadium.

Then the next day, number two met number one.

It was an execution of precision. With Duke Carlisle operating the Royal Winged-T offense to perfection and the defense hammering the Sooners, Texas won, 28–7. A sportswriter from St. Louis perhaps told the story best when he wrote in his lead, "Who's No. 1? It is Texas, podner, and smile when you say that. . . . "

Texas then began the improbable challenge of carrying the nation's number-one ranking for six long weeks. It made it through tough wins over Arkansas (17–13), Rice (10–6), SMU (17–12), Baylor (7–0), TCU (17–0), and Texas A&M (15–13).

The Baylor game, matching the unbeaten Horns against a Baylor team led by Don Trull and Lawrence Elkins, had been the best showdown in years in the Southwest Conference. Late in the game Carlisle intercepted a sure touchdown, saving the Longhorn victory.

With an open date between the TCU and Texas A&M games, Darrell Royal was standing in his bedroom, tying his tie, getting ready for the events of the afternoon.

It was Friday, November 22.

At Austin's Municipal Auditorium, the crystal glasses and silverware were all in place, as the seal of the President of the United States adorned the speaker's podium, waiting for a dinner that would never happen. At a campus hangout called Fritz's, students lunched and grabbed a quick beer as suddenly, somebody ran to the bar to listen to the radio. First one, and then another.

"Must be something about the president," someone said. "You know he's coming to Austin this afternoon after his speech in Dallas."

Royal, who was to meet President John F. Kennedy when his flight landed in Austin, got the word as he was dressing to go meet the plane.

"I was the person chosen to welcome him to Austin," Royal said. "He had learned how to do the 'Hook 'em Horns' sign and was prepared to flash it as I shook his hand. I went into our living room and just sat stunned until Walter Cronkite came on TV and said that the president had died."

The shots fired in Dallas reverberated around the world, but particularly so in Austin. On the UT campus, the president had been popular, even in the state of his chief Democratic opponent, vice president Lyndon Johnson. Now, Johnson, by virtue of an assassin's bullet, was president. The Texas governor, John Connally, a former student body president at UT, had been seriously wounded.

Royal, who had become friends with both men, was faced with a dilemma. College football games that weekend were canceled, but the Longhorns and Texas A&M were scheduled to play the most important game of Royal's career—and perhaps in Texas history—six days later on Thanksgiving Day.

For the first time, national live television became a major factor in America's life. We saw the man accused of killing the president gunned down in the basement of a courthouse before our very eyes and watched as the dream of the new order and "Camelot" faded with a little boy's salute to his daddy's casket.

Now, less than a week later, life dictated that it must, somehow, go on.

Thanksgiving Day, November 28, dawned cold and dreary in College Station. The field, which had been dampened with rain, was made even worse when the grounds crew brought in dirt that quickly turned the surface into a quagmire.

The Color of Orange

The season of 1928 brought a Southwest Conference championship to Texas, but it also brought the beginning of a Longhorn tradition. Prior to that season, Texas had worn bright orange jerseys, which faded badly in laundering. In fact, the color became so washed out that opponents derisively referred to the Longhorns as "yellow bellies."

Head coach Clyde Littlefield had a friend, a Mr. O'Shea of the O'Shea Knitting Mills in Chicago. When he told O'Shea of the problem, he promised to "work up some different colored yarn."

"When we get you the color of orange you like," historian Lou Maysel quotes Littlefield as remembering O'Shea saying, "we're gonna establish it as your orange."

The color O'Shea and Littlefield came up with was a darker, rust-colored "burnt orange," and it became recognized in the sporting good business as "Texas Orange."

Texas stayed with the color until World War II, when it had to go to a lighter color because the dyes for the burnt orange were made in Germany and weren't available, for obvious reasons.

In the early 1960s, Darrell Royal got together with Rooster Andrews, who represented a sporting goods company at the time (he later would own his own company), and in 1962 Royal brought back the burnt orange color to Longhorn uniforms.

When Mack Brown came to Texas as the Longhorn football coach in 1998, he exhorted fans to "Come early, be loud, stay late, and wear orange with pride," and the idea took off. By 2005, Texas was second only to Notre Dame in school-related apparel sold nationally.

And just as it appeared Texas was on the verge of that first-ever national championship, Texas A&M held onto a 13–9 lead in the closing minutes of the season finale. As hopes began to dim, Texas A&M intercepted a Texas pass but fumbled on the return when they inexplicably tried to lateral the ball. Tom Stockton, the fullback who had scored the only touchdown in

End Charlie Talbert (89) signals a touchdown as Duke Carlisle (11) scores to give Texas a hard-fought victory over Texas A&M, clinching the Longhorns' first national championship in 1963.

the Baylor game, recovered to give Texas new life. Then, as Texas zeroed in on the goal line, another Aggie tipped a Texas pass and gained control only after he had fallen out of the end zone, missing what would have been a game-saving interception. A photographer named Jim Seymour captured the descriptive picture of the defender's knee ruts, where he landed just beyond the end zone line.

Finally, Carlisle plunged over from the 1 yard line, and Texas prevailed. The national championship was accomplished. The polls crowned Texas as champions at the end of the regular season, but there were doubters in the media in the eastern part of the country. Navy, which had lost only that game to SMU in Dallas back in October, openly challenged the Longhorns' ranking.

Wayne Hardin, the coach of the Naval Academy, had lobbied for a post–bowl game decision. On the field before the game, Hardin told a national TV commentator in an interview broadcast across the nation as well as to the crowd in the stands, "When the challenger meets the champion and the challenger wins, then there is a new champion."

To which Royal answered a crisp, "We're ready."

Despite owning three national championship recognitions, Texas was almost the underdog going into the game. The Longhorns were lambasted as "fraud," and "unable to pass," and generally not what they were cracked up to be.

Finally, on top of all the publicity, Royal spoke back to the critics.

"Look," he said in obvious ire, "we're not a darned bit afraid to put it on the line."

Hardin's strategy was to make Texas pass, and the Longhorns did. The Midshipmen came out in an eight-man line, which left gaping holes in the secondary for Carlisle to exploit. And he did, setting a Cotton Bowl total offense record and earning all but one vote as the game's outstanding back. Texas actually held a 21–0 lead at one point and finished the game with its reserves on the field, a yard away from another score at the Navy goal line.

Texas hammered the Midshipmen, 28–6, and Staubach would say years later that the hardest he was ever hit, as a quarterback in college or during his illustrious career with the Dallas Cowboys, was in that Cotton Bowl game.

Allison Danzig, the respected writer for the *New York Times*, summed up the game pretty well.

"The first University of Texas football team ever to be recognized as national intercollegiate champion sealed its claim to preeminence today with an overwhelming 28–6 victory over Navy in the Cotton Bowl.

"Roger Staubach, Heisman Trophy winner and the most celebrated player of the year in leading Navy to a ranking second only to Texas, was harried unmercifully and eclipsed by Duke Carlisle as the Texas quarterback threw two tremendous touchdown passes and scored one touchdown in one of the most shining performances on record in the New Year's Day fixture."

Joe Trimble of the *New York Daily News* added, "Texas brags. But they're entitled to talk big. The powerful Longhorns clearly proved their right to No. 1 rank in the nation today when they thoroughly thrashed second ranked Navy, 28–6, in the 28th Cotton Bowl."

Namath and Nobis

One of the best games in the Darrell Royal era at Texas is often overlooked in discussions of famous victories, because it came after the regular season and in a bowl game that didn't affect Texas's national ranking.

But all the same, the 1965 Orange Bowl was a classic much like the Longhorns 2005 victory in the Rose Bowl.

The Longhorns were matched against Alabama, which had already clinched a national championship, since the polls had awarded the trophy after the 1964 regular season.

The Crimson Tide, led by quarterback Joe Namath, were installed as a six-point favorite prior to the first-ever New Year's Night bowl game. By game time, however, the margin was down to three points because Namath had reinjured a knee that would trouble him throughout his later career in professional football.

The Longhorns had jumped to a 21–17 lead, thanks to a 79-yard touchdown run by Ernie Koy Jr. and a 69-yard pass from Jim Hudson to George Sauer, both of whom, ironically, would go on to play with Namath in professional ball for the New York Jets.

The game turned on a pivotal goal-line stand. With just over six minutes remaining in the game, Alabama had first and goal from the Texas 6 yard line. The Tide gained 4 yards on the first play, but two line plunges netted only 1 more yard. On fourth down, Namath tried a quarterback sneak. Texas tackle Tom Currie disrupted the play, linebacker Frank Bedrick hit Namath at the line, and as the Alabama quarterback tried to slide off, the Longhorns All-America linebacker Tommy Nobis stopped him cold, just short of the goal.

The victory changed little on the national scene, since Alabama had been crowned national champ by both the Associated Press and UPI. The Longhorns' Southwest Conference foe Arkansas picked up a couple of second-tier awards as number one after the bowl games. Texas concluded its season at 10–1, completing a remarkable four-year run with a record of 40–2–1.

And finally from George Minot of the *Washington Post*, "The winner and still collegiate football champion of the world—Texas. Advertised as the title game between the nation's number one and number two ranked teams, the 28th Cotton Bowl Classic was turned into a shambles by a rampaging Longhorn line and a quarterback who they said couldn't pass, but did."

On the season, Tommy Ford and Scott Appleton each earned All-America honors, and they were joined by a young sophomore named Tommy Nobis, who gained the first of his three years of national recognition. The heroes were legion. When their tenure on the Forty Acres was finished, the seniors of 1963 had posted an incredible three-year record of 30–2–1.

Looking back, the most remarkable thing about the season of 1963 was the closeness of the games, yet except for the frightening moments late in the Aggie game, one never had the feeling that the team was threatened.

But in the short span of their college days, life as they had known it changed.

Just as the 1941 team will forever be linked with the events of December 7 that year, so the fall of 1963 was to be remembered more for tragedy than it was for football. A year before, the missiles of October in Cuba had given them their first taste of actual fear, as the country and the world stood on the brink of war, and there were stirrings of a conflict in some faraway place called Vietnam. But when President Kennedy was killed in Dallas, we were all forever changed.

Today, elevators are run by computers, and all doors have exit bars and keys. The hole in the stadium where the old door was is now full of video cables and concrete. Our world is one of caution, and security is a device in an airport or a search at the stadium gate.

But in the chambers of the mind, on a fall evening where you can see the stars and remember, there was a team that made Texas proud and won it all and set a standard that opened the way for more.

And in that space, in the memory of a time gone by, we are once again safe.

The Wishbone

Emory Bellard sat in his office, down the narrow, eggshell-white corridor that was part of an annex linking old Gregory Gymnasium with a recreational facility for students. There were two exit doors, one at the glassed-in front of the two-story building, and the other at the end of the hall.

Summer in 1968 was a time for football coaches to relax and to prepare for the upcoming season. Most of Bellard's cohorts on Darrell

Royal's staff were either on vacation or had finished their work in the morning and were spending the afternoon at the golf course at old Austin Country Club.

Texas football had taken a sabbatical from the elite of the college ranks in the three previous years. From the time Tommy Nobis and Darrell Royal's 1964 team had beaten Joe Namath and Alabama in the first night bowl game, the Orange Bowl on January 1 of 1965, Longhorn football had leveled to average. Three seasons of 6–4, 7–4, and 6–4 had followed the exceptional run in the early 1960s.

Despite an outstanding running back in future College Football Hall of Famer Chris Gilbert, the popular I formation with a single running back hadn't produced as Royal and his staff had hoped. So with the coming of the 1968 season, and the influx of a highly touted freshman class who would be sophomores (this was before freshmen were eligible to play on the varsity), Royal had made a switch in coaching duties.

Bellard, who had joined the staff only a season before, after a successful career in Texas high-school coaching at San Angelo and Breckenridge, was the new offensive backfield coach.

Bellard had gone to Royal with the idea of switching to the Veer, an option offense that had become popular in the southwest at the University of Houston. As the Longhorns had gone through spring training, they had returned to the Winged-T formation that Royal had used so successfully during the early part of the decade.

So, as the summer began, the ongoing question was, who was going to play fullback, the veteran Ted Koy or the sensational sophomore newcomer Steve Worster? With Gilbert a fixture at

Being Koy

No family has contributed more to Longhorn football than that of Ernie Koy Sr., who became part of a legendary backfield along with Hall of Fame member Harrison Stafford in the early 1930s.

In 1962 Koy's oldest son, Ernie Jr., became an outstanding punter and running back for Darrell Royal's Longhorns. Despite battling injuries, he was a significant factor in the early success in the 1960s for Texas. His young brother, Ted, entered the picture in 1967 and was a star running back in the Wishbone on the national championship team of 1969.

Both Ernie Jr. and Ted went on to successful careers in pro football. The patriarch of the family, Ernie Sr., became a professional baseball star, playing in the golden era of the National League for the Brooklyn Dodgers in the 1930s.

running back, even in the two-back set of the Veer formation, only one of the other two could play.

And that is how, on that summer afternoon, the conversation began.

"So, who are you going to play, Koy or Worster?" the question was asked. Bellard took a draw on his ever-present pipe, cocked his chair a little behind the desk that faced the door, and said, "What if we play them both?" He took out a yellow pad and drew four circles in a shape resembling the letter Y.

"Bradley," he said, referring to heralded quarterback Bill Bradley, as he pointed to the bottom of the picture. "Worster," he said, indicating a position at the juncture behind the quarterback. "Koy," he said as he dotted the right side, "and Gilbert," indicating the left halfback.

Royal had told Bellard he wanted a formation that would be balanced, and that—unlike the Veer, which was a two-back set— would employ a triple option with a lead blocker. On summer mornings, Bellard would set up the alignments inside the old gymnasium next to the offices, using volunteers from the athletics staff as players.

As fall drills began, the formation was kept under wraps. Ironically, Texas opened the season that year against Houston. It was only the second meeting of the two. The Longhorns had won easily in 1953, but the Cougars had established themselves as an independent power that was demanding respect from the old guard Southwest Conference.

A packed house of more than 66,000 overflowed Texas Memorial Stadium for the game, which ended in a 20–20 tie. The debut of the new formation didn't exactly shock the football world.

A week later, Texas headed to Texas Tech for its first conference game and found itself trailing 21–0 in the first half. It was at that point that Royal made the first of a series of moves that would change the face of his offense and the face of college football, for that matter.

Bill Bradley was the most celebrated athlete in Texas in the mid-1960s. He was a football quarterback and a baseball player; he could throw with either hand and could punt with either foot. He was a senior, and when Royal unveiled the new formation, he

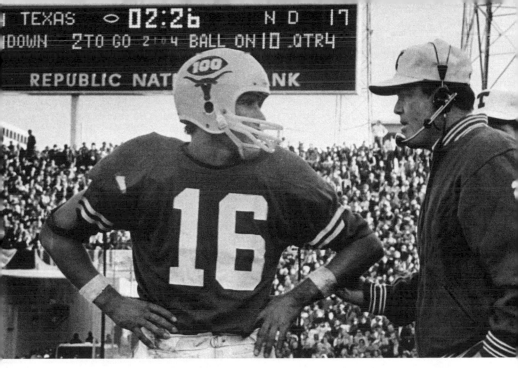

James Street and Darrell Royal discuss a critical fourth down call late in the 1970 Cotton Bowl.

thought that Bradley's running ability would make him perfect as the quarterback who would pull the trigger.

But trailing in Lubbock, Royal made one of the hardest decisions of his coaching career. He pulled Bradley and inserted a little-known junior named James Street.

A signal caller from Longview, Texas, Street had been an All-Southwest Conference pitcher in baseball the spring before, but no one could have expected what was about to happen.

Street brought Texas back to within striking distance of the Raiders, closing the gap to 28–22 before Tech eventually won, 31–22.

Back home in Austin, the staff met to adjust where the players lined up in the new formation. In a debate that was won by offensive line coach Willie Zapalac, the fullback alignment was adjusted. Worster, who had been lined up only a yard behind the quarterback in the original formation, was moved back two full steps so he could better see the holes the line had created as the play developed.

Against Oklahoma State the next week, Texas won, 31–3. Nobody realized it at the time, but that would be the start of something very big. With Street as the signal caller, that win was the first of thirty straight victories, the most in the NCAA since Oklahoma had set a national record in the 1950s, and a string that held as the nation's best for more than thirty years.

While the Oklahoma State game started the streak, the Oklahoma game the next week would become known as "The Game That Made the Wishbone."

Texas was 1–1–1 as it headed to Dallas to play the Sooners, and with only 2:37 remaining in the game, Street and Royal's new offense were at their own 15 yard line, trailing 20–19. A legend was about to be born. Street hooked up with tight end Deryl Comer for pass completions of 18, 21, and 13 yards, and then connected with Bradley, who had moved to split end after the Tech game, for 10 yards to the Oklahoma 21 yard line. Only 55 seconds remained as Worster crashed through a big hole to the 7.

On the sidelines, assistant coach R. M. Patterson corralled a wide-eyed Happy Feller, his sophomore field-goal kicker, and told him that if the Longhorns didn't score a touchdown on the next play, he was going to have to hurry out and kick, because Texas was out of time-outs.

While Texas was struggling on the field in the mid-1960s, the recruiting season of 1967 had netted the most successful recruit-

Easy Street

Few players in Texas history have ever captured the admiration of Longhorn fans as did James Street, who quarterbacked the Longhorns to a national championship in 1969 and earned All-America honors as a baseball pitcher as well.

Street, who never lost as a Texas starting quarterback in twenty games, would also come back in the national collegiate sports picture more than thirty years after he finished his career as a Longhorn, but this time, he'd do it as a featured spectator.

In 2002 one of his five sons, Huston, followed in Dad's footsteps to stardom. Huston led the Longhorn baseball team to the NCAA College World Series title, earning four saves and being named the tournament's Most Valuable Player.

ing haul in Southwest Conference history. The linchpin of the group was Steve Worster, a powerful running back from Bridge City. The recruiting class would forever be known as The Worster Crowd.

With time running out at the Oklahoma 7 yard line, James Street handed the ball to Steve Worster. Two Sooners tried to stop him, but the bruising fullback who was on his way to stardom dragged them with him as he dived into the end zone. Only 39 seconds remained. Texas won, 26–20. The next week the Longhorns pounded Arkansas.

In one of his postgame meetings with the sportswriters at the Villa Capri Motor Hotel (which stood where the UT indoor practice facility is located today) following the game, a writer asked Royal what he called the new offense.

"I don't know," he said. "What do you guys think?"

Mickey Herskowitz of the *Houston Post* followed several other suggestions by saying, "Well, it looks like a chicken 'pully-bone.'"

"Okay," said Royal. "The Wishbone."

The new-fangled offense would team with a solid Longhorn defense to dominate the era. Street would record the best win-loss record as a quarterback in Texas history, starting twenty games and winning all of them.

The 1968 team would finish fifth in the country, pounding number eight Tennessee, 36–13, in the Cotton Bowl. The offense had become unstoppable. Following the 20–20 tie with Houston in the season opener, Cougar coach Bill Yeoman had told the media, "I wish we had a chance to play them again." That prompted irreverent sportswriters to comment at halftime of the New Year's Day game in Dallas, "Somebody call Yeoman and tell him to bring his team on up . . . this thing is over."

The season of 1969 was the centennial year of college football. In 1869 Princeton and Rutgers had played in the first game ever, and the NCAA had chosen to celebrate the anniversary. Each collegiate team was given a patch signifying "100," and the Longhorns chose to wear theirs on their helmets, in the cradle of the two horns on the school's emblem.

Beano Cook, who was an executive with the NCAA's television partner ABC, suggested that the network find an appropriate game to move to the end of the season, as the climax to the centennial year. The game he landed on was the Texas-Arkansas game in Fayetteville, which was regularly scheduled for the third week in October. The two schools agreed and moved their October 18 date to December 6.

No one could have envisioned how successful Cook's idea would become.

When Texas beat Texas Tech on September 27, the Longhorns moved to number two in the polls. But Ohio State was the defending national champion, and the Buckeyes showed every indication they would repeat. For six weeks, the two remained number one and number two.

Texas's final regular-season game normally would have been against Texas A&M, and after playing TCU on November 15,

The Longhorns putting their Wishbone offense to good use in a 1970 game.

Texas had an open date until their Thanksgiving Day meeting with the Aggies on November 27.

On Saturday, November 22, Royal took a "busman's holiday" and headed to Waco to watch SMU and Baylor play. Far away in Ann Arbor, Michigan, the Wolverines, under first-year coach Bo Schembechler, were stunning Ohio State, 24–12.

Suddenly Texas was number one, and Arkansas rose to number two. Beano Cook, who had envisioned only a good game to close the centennial year of college football, now had one for the ages. And Fayetteville, Arkansas, was about to become the center of the college football universe.

The hype of the game took on epic proportions. With the network and the NCAA promoting the game, President Richard Nixon joined in the excitement. It was announced that he would attend the game and present a Presidential Plaque to the winner, recognizing them as the national champion in the one hundredth year of college football. Renowned preacher Billy Graham gave the pregame invocation.

Heading into the game, both teams appeared healthy and ready, except perhaps for Texas's little junior safety Freddie Steinmark, who was trying to hide a limp from his coaches, a malady caused, he thought, by a hip bruise.

It was cold, bone cold that drizzly day in Fayetteville. And that day, lives were changed forever because of a football game. The night before the game, an icy drizzle rattled on the roof of the Holiday Inn in Rodgers, Arkansas, where the Texas team was staying. The field was one of the new artificial surfaces called AstroTurf, and both teams struggled to find shoes that would get good traction on the surface, which fluctuated between wet and dry. On the forty-five-minute bus ride to the stadium, Royal looked out at the flashing red lights of the Arkansas State Police car leading the team, and to pass the time, he called Street to join him at the front of the bus. He surprised his quarterback by telling him what he wanted to do if the Longhorns trailed by fourteen points late in the game. "When we score the first time, I want to go for two and here's the play I want you to run."

It would not be the last time Royal would surprise Street that day. Even though the senior signal caller thought there was no chance Texas would be in such a dire situation, Street dutifully noted Royal's wish.

The game had not gone well for Texas. The Longhorns were plagued by turnovers, and Arkansas held a surprising 14–0 lead as the third quarter ended.

On the first play of the fourth quarter, Street dropped back to pass but couldn't find an open receiver. Not known for his blazing speed, he dodged a would-be tackler and somehow outran the Razorbacks 42 yards to the goal line.

The score was 14–6. A tie would have put the Razorbacks—as league cochamps—in the Cotton Bowl, since the Longhorns had been the year before. It also would have ended Texas's dream of the national championship. So just as he had envisioned on the bus, Royal went for two. Street wasted no time in calling the predetermined play (an option left), and when he cut in off left guard and into the end zone for the successful conversion, it was 14–8.

Arkansas quarterback Bill Montgomery would mount a fourth-quarter drive that would bring the Razorbacks within field-goal range midway through the period. Pass interference was called when Steinmark reached out and caught hold of Arkansas receiver Chuck Dicus when he was surprisingly beaten on a play that would likely have been a touchdown.

Montgomery was at the Texas 7 yard line when Arkansas coach Frank Broyles sent in a call that Razorback offensive coach Don Breaux had made from the press box, a call that will live in infamy forever in Arkansas. On third down, only a chip-shot field goal away from an insurmountable 17–8 lead, Montgomery rolled left to pass. A Razorback receiver waited in the end zone, but as Montgomery threw, Texas halfback Danny Lester stepped in front and intercepted the ball and ran it out to the 20.

But the breath that Texas had been given seemed on life support a series later, when 4:47 remained in the game and Street walked to the sidelines to talk with Royal. It was fourth down, 3 yards to go, and the ball was at the Texas 43 yard line. A packed stadium and an estimated television audience of twenty-eight million watched.

It was then that Street got his second surprise of the day from Royal. The choices seemed fairly simple. First, there was Worster up the middle. But Texas had found trouble running against the Razorbacks all day. Street himself had turned the option up for the two-point conversion, but the center of the field was slippery, and Arkansas would expect a running play. Cotton Speyrer was the Longhorns top receiver, and a short pass to him seemed the most logical selection to Bellard, who was calling plays in the press box, as well as to Street.

At halftime, Randy Peschel, the Longhorns tight end, had told Royal that the Arkansas secondary was meeting him in close to the line of scrimmage. "I think I can get behind them if we need it," he had said. And that, Royal determined, was exactly what Texas needed right now.

Stepping-Stones

Not only did Darrell Royal succeed with his players, he also pro-moted great success in his assistant coaches during his twenty years with the Longhorns. Of Royal's first staff, four of the origi-nal seven went on to become head coaches. Ray Willsey (Califor-nia), Jack Swarthout (Montana), Jim Pittman (Tulane and TCU), and Charley Shira (Mississippi State) came off of Royal's initial staff. Later, Emory Bellard (Texas A&M and Mississippi State), Fred Akers (Wyoming and Texas), David McWilliams (Texas Tech and Texas), and Spike Dykes (Texas Tech) earned head coaching positions after having been a part of Royal's Texas staff.

"Run 53 Veer Pass," Royal said. The play called for Peschel to run a deep flag pattern. Mike Campbell, Royal's valued friend and defensive coordinator, heard the call and jumped back.

"Darrell," he said. "There's only one receiver out, and he's deep. It's all or nothing."

"Fifty-three Veer Pass," Royal repeated.

Campbell turned and gathered his defense around him.

"Get ready," he said. "We're fixin' to give them the ball at our own 43, and we've got to stop 'em one more time."

Street turned as he headed onto the field and walked back toward Royal.

"Coach, are you sure that's the play you want?" he asked. Emphatically, Royal told him that it was.

Texas had believed that the Razorback defense was studying the Texas huddle throughout the game, trying to pick up any sign they could. So Street, when he got in the huddle, looked straight at Speyrer.

"I'm looking at you, Cotton, but I am talking to you, Randy," he said. "You guys aren't going to believe this play, but it is gonna work."

History records it as perhaps the most significant play in Texas history. Peschel barely got a step on the Razorback defender, and Street threw a perfect pass that hit him in stride at the Arkansas 13 yard line. Through the fog and icy mist, Texas had made the play of the game in the Game of the Century. On the next snap, Ted Koy followed the block of Bobby Wuensch 11 yards to the 2. It was the longest rushing gain for Texas on the day. Jim Bertelsen, a sophomore who had taken Chris Gilbert's left halfback position when Gilbert graduated, scored the touchdown.

Feller, who R. M. Patterson thought might have been nervous as a sophomore against Oklahoma, booted the extra point that gave Texas a 15–14 lead. But Arkansas had 3:58 in which to answer. They were at the Texas 39 yard line when the drama finally ended. Tom Campbell, one of the twin sons of Campbell the coach, intercepted Montgomery at the Longhorn 21 with 1:22 on the clock. Texas ran out the final few seconds.

In the crowded locker room in a grey concrete building, Texas celebrated. Nixon presented Royal and the team captains with the plaque.

As Texas left the stadium, snowflakes fell gently on the team buses as they made their way through the Ozark Mountains, 50 miles to Fort Smith, where they could catch the plane home.

A crowd of 10,000 fans swarmed onto the runway when the team arrived in Austin. Street, who was claustrophobic, stayed on the plane until everybody else had moved away from the stairs.

What Texas had earned was not only the national championship and the SWC title, it had achieved the right to be a part of even more history. After more than forty years, since the days of the famed Four Horsemen, Notre Dame agreed to play the Longhorns in the Cotton Bowl game. Things could not have been more jubilant for Texas football, but all that was about to change.

Freddie Steinmark, the young safety who had perhaps saved the game by interfering with a receiver, still was bothered by the

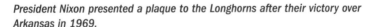

President Nixon presented a plaque to the Longhorns after their victory over Arkansas in 1969.

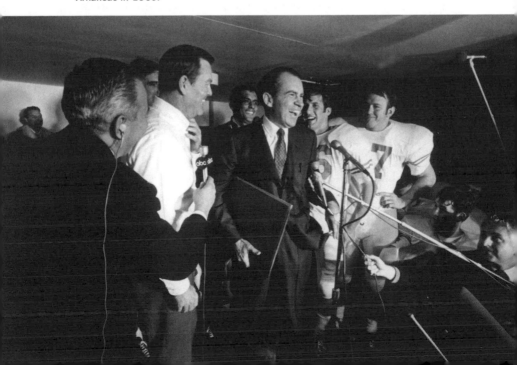

hip injury. On Tuesday doctors discovered the cause of the pain: He had a huge tumor in his hip. Friday, less than a week after the victory, his leg was removed because of bone cancer.

The disease, at the time, was almost always fatal. But Steinmark wasn't willing to give up. He beat the odds by walking down the tunnel into the Cotton Bowl three weeks later for the game against Notre Dame, and he stood on the sidelines the whole time as Street and Worster and Koy and Speyrer and the Texas defense and Tom Campbell worked their magic one final time. A fourth-down pass, this time from the Irish 10 to the 2, had set up the game-winning touchdown. Tom Campbell's interception of Joe Theisman's pass sealed the 21–17 victory.

In the locker room, Royal and the team gave the game ball to Steinmark. A year and a half later, the spunky safety lost his battle with cancer. He died in June of 1971. The scoreboard in the stadium in Austin was dedicated to his memory, and when Mack Brown came to Texas to coach in 1998, he established a tradition that calls for all players to touch Steinmark's picture on the scoreboard before they enter the field. He told them to do it to remind them of the courage that Freddie showed in his battle for life.

Street was gone, but with Eddie Phillips guiding the Wishbone, the Longhorns of 1970 would pull off a miracle win over UCLA and go on to extend the winning streak to thirty games before finally falling in the Cotton Bowl in a rematch with Notre Dame on New Year's Day, 1971. That team, however, earned the Horns third national championship when the UPI Coaches' trophy was presented at the end of the regular season.

Teams all over the country experimented with Royal's creative formation, and Bear Bryant at Alabama and Chuck Fairbanks at Oklahoma would install versions of it that would lead to more national championships.

Royal would stick with the formation until he retired from coaching in 1976, winning four Southwest Conference titles over those next six seasons.

While it was a significant era in college football, Royal's legacy would best be remembered for the two dramatic victories that closed the 1969 season. To that point, his reputation had been as a conservative, run-oriented coach who once made famous the saying, "Only three things can happen when you pass, and two of them are bad."

Royal had said it as a joke, but the reputation stuck.

After the victory over Notre Dame in the Cotton Bowl, a senior citizen was running the old hand-operated elevator that went to the press box in the stadium on the State Fair Grounds. A writer coming back from the dressing room climbed aboard for a trip back to the top.

"I'll tell you one thing," said the old man, shaking his head and thinking of the fourth-down calls against the Razorbacks and Irish. "I wouldn't want to get into a card game with that Darrell Royal . . . boy, is he a riverboat gambler. . . . "

The "wishbone" is a cut of the best white meat in a fried chicken, and what remained after the meat was devoured was a bone shaped like the letter V. Kids would fight for the right to pull the bone apart. You would make a wish, and if you got lucky on the bone break, you supposedly got your wish.

And in the late 1960s, Darrell Royal and the Longhorns obviously chose wisely as they reached for the pully-bone and grasped a brass ring.

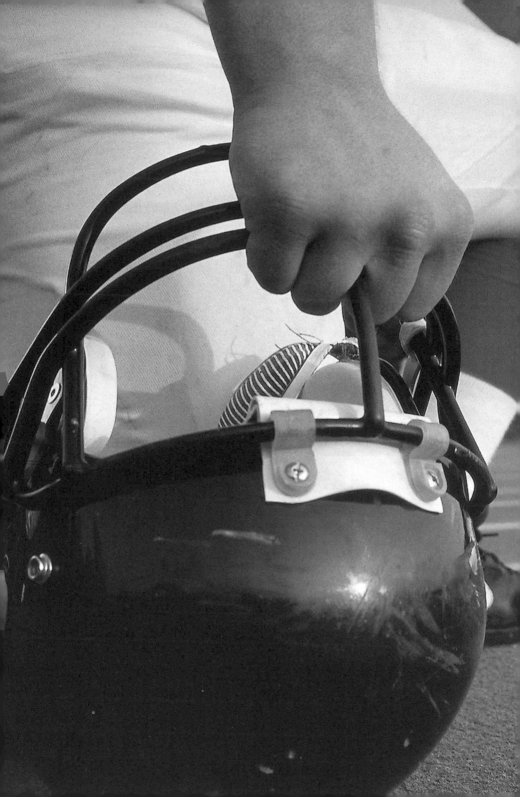

The Longhorn Heismans

At the end, they said you could still see the Statue of Liberty through the crack in the window on the thirteenth floor of the building at 19 West Street, on the banks where the Hudson River leans toward the Atlantic Ocean at the edge of downtown New York City. The tattered awning shielded the closed entrance, the words HOME OF THE HEISMAN barely visible.

The Downtown Athletic Club was closing its doors after seventy-three years, shattered beyond repair by the blasts that took down the twin towers of the World Trade Center a couple of years before.

The thirteenth floor was important in a building that had thirty-eight stories of hotel rooms, gymnasiums, meeting rooms, and a swimming pool. Its once-rich red carpet was covered with dust at the end, a distant memory away from the way it was all dressed up in 1998.

For it was in December each year that the Downtown Athletic Club polished the brass, put up the Christmas tree in the lobby, and got ready as the college football world made a pilgrimage to its doors. As the tree glowed, so a new star's portrait was hung on the thirteenth floor.

It was in that moment, on that special December day in 1998, that Ricky Williams and Earl Campbell were permanently linked in Texas football lore. For as finalists for the award, media and friends and family gathered there in the Heisman room, Williams joined Campbell as Texas Longhorns who had won the most prestigious award in college football.

They were products of a different time, with different stories. Yet now, they were forever joined in history.

"Funny," says our old friend Willie Nelson, "how time slips away."

It was the summer of 1977, as the smartly dressed player and the new coach rode the elevator to the top of what was then called Memorial Stadium and took a picture for the cover of the UT football media guide.

The massive books that are produced now weren't even a

dream in those days. The "Press Guide," as it was called, was 4 inches by 9 inches—a pocket-size pamphlet of 104 pages.

The photo on the cover was only about 4 inches square, but it was important to be current, so the new head coach and star player rode with the photographer up to the eleventh floor, unlocked the gate to the stadium, and posed in the stands with the stadium field and the LBJ Library in the background.

There they were, dressed in suits and looking all spiffed up for the "new beginning" of Texas football. The picture turned out pretty well, and as the book got ready to go to press, a cutline was added at the bottom of the picture that read, "Head Coach Fred Akers, Heisman Candidate Earl Campbell."

Heisman candidate?

That was a pretty big stretch for a guy who hadn't even made the all-conference team the year before. Other folks were just beginning the glitzy campaigns promoting candidates, but that one sentence on that little guide was the only published piece of literature proclaiming that Earl Campbell might be the best player in college football in 1977.

Earl Campbell was famous long before he stepped on the field to play football for Darrell Royal at Texas. His high school career at Tyler (John Tyler) was the stuff from which legends are made. He was, to those who saw him, the greatest high school running back in state history. And while over thirty years have passed since he claimed that title as a senior in 1973, people around East Texas will tell you it is a title he still holds.

They write books and sing songs about guys like Earl Campbell. The most powerful person in his life was his mama, Ann Campbell, who raised roses to earn the money to feed her eleven kids after Earl's dad died when Earl was just past ten years old.

He would become the "Tyler Rose," and the recruiting of Earl Campbell was one of the most spirited competitions of the spring of 1974. Ken Dabbs, a Texas assistant who had been a fine high school coach, was the point person for Darrell Royal's staff, and he was matched against the best from every school in the country.

But whatever the challenge, or the illegal offers Earl faced, it was Mama Campbell who would stand in the doorway, fending off the other folks. Once, when she had been sent to bed because of high blood pressure, Earl came in the room around 9:30 one evening. It seemed that Barry Switzer, the head coach at Oklahoma, wanted to come over and visit. Dabbs was in the house at the time.

"You tell them 'no,'" Dabbs remembers Ann Campbell saying. "You know you want to go down to Texas with Coach Dabbs. And besides, those Oklahoma coaches are the reason I am lying here in this bed right now."

In a time when illegal payments to recruits were fairly common, Earl dug deep in his roots to refuse them.

"No," he would say defiantly. "My people have been bought and sold long enough."

And so it was that in the spring of 1974, Earl Campbell signed to become a Texas Longhorn.

It was a brave choice for a young African-American player. The University of Texas had long fought the image of being a racist institution, ever since the days of a young black law student named Heman Sweatt. Long before James Meredith became famous for trying to break the color line at the University of

Earl Campbell became the Longhorns' all-time touchdown leader during his bid for the Heisman Trophy in 1977.

Mississippi, Sweatt filed a lawsuit against UT that would be the landmark case for integration.

As other schools such as Oklahoma integrated their football teams in the 1950s, the teams of the Southwest Conference lagged behind until 1965, when the league, and therefore The University of Texas, officially declared an end to the policy of segregation. Still, it didn't become a reality at Texas until the late 1960s; in 1970 a young lineman named Julius Whittier became the first African-American letterman at Texas. Still, the racist image stuck, despite Royal's best efforts to dispute it, until a young man named Roosevelt Leaks came to play fullback at Texas in 1971.

Where Whittier had succeeded, Leaks would excel. Where Whittier was a low profile offensive lineman and tight end, Leaks would be a star. Freshmen weren't eligible for the varsity in 1971, but when Leaks moved to the starting lineup as a sophomore in 1972, he changed the face of Texas football. When he finished third in the Heisman Trophy voting as a junior in 1973, he shattered the myth that a young black man would not be allowed to play at Texas. That same fall, Earl Campbell was becoming a larger-than-life legend in high school football. In the recruiting coup of the 1970s, Earl Campbell signed to become a Texas Longhorn.

His success was immediate. Freshmen had become eligible to play on the varsity in 1972, and Leaks, the All-America running back, was battling to come back from knee surgery after a spring practice injury. Campbell became the fullback in the Texas Wishbone. He gained 928 yards and helped lead the team to the Gator Bowl. As he prepared for a sophomore season where he would lead Texas to a Southwest Conference tri-championship, he sat down in the Sports Information Office for one of the most memorable interviews ever.

"What makes you run?" he was asked.

"I want to be a pro football player. I want to be successful in what I try to do. It is part of me, just like the clothes I wear. The way I look at it, it's a gift that God gave me and this is what I am meant to do. I want to make it so I can help take care of my family. I want to buy my mama a house so she won't have to look at the stars at night through the holes in the roof. And after I have done that, maybe I can be of help to some who are less fortunate than I."

And then, at just twenty years of age, he continued talking.

"I try each night to read the Bible, and I say my prayers. People wonder how I get out there and run like I do. On game days, especially on game days, I sit on the bench, I put on that suit, and I say a prayer. I remember a sign in my high school dressing room that said, 'A quitter never wins, and a winner never quits.' I think about that all the time. There are times when I feel like I want to quit, but whenever I do, I just say a little prayer and suddenly my day is brighter.

"If it weren't for the dark days, we wouldn't know what it is to walk in the light."

He was named an All-American that sophomore season and then struggled throughout 1976—Darrell Royal's last year—with a hamstring injury. The trainers and the doctors knew what was the matter, but they had problems getting to the source to treat the injury. The pulled hamstring was buried deep within Earl's thigh, which measured an incredible 30 inches . . . more than a lot of college students' waists.

A Star-crossed Career

In the first seven years of his ten-year career at Texas, Fred Akers posted the best winning percentage of any coach in Southwest Conference history. But destiny never seemed to smile on Akers and his teams.

Twice, in 1977 and 1983, he came within a game of winning a national championship, as his teams posted two 11–1 seasons. In his first seven seasons, he finished in the nation's top five three times. His teams were 66–17–1 through his first seven seasons. But in a Southwest Conference hit heavily by recruiting scandals, Akers's teams finished 7–4–1 in 1984, 8–4 in 1985, and finally 5–6 in his last year of 1986.

His overall record at Texas was 86–31–2 (60–19–1 in the SWC), second only to Darrell Royal in victories. He took his team to nine bowl games, coached a Heisman Trophy winner in Earl Campbell, an Outland Trophy honoree (Brad Shearer), and two Lombardi winners (Kenneth Sims and Tony Degrate).

After leaving Texas, Akers finished his coaching career at Purdue, before returning to his ranch near Austin.

But when that picture was taken in the summer of 1977, things had changed. Fred Akers had installed the "I" formation, with Earl as the tailback. And the season upon which they were about to embark would be like a tale from a storybook.

The Texas Sports Information Office developed the statistic of YAC, or Yards After Contact. It is common today, but Texas was the first to use it to reflect the power of a running back. Earl, who gained more than two-thirds of his yards after being hit by an opponent, set conference and school rushing records, and he led the NCAA with 1,744 yards and 114 points.

Coach Royal had told him in his freshman year to always play with class. When other players were dancing and showboating after big plays (before the NCAA outlawed such behavior), Coach Royal told Earl, "Earl, when you get in that end zone, act like you have been there before."

And Earl was in there a lot.

He led the Horns to an 11–0 record and a number one ranking at the end of the regular season. Only an upset by Notre Dame in the Cotton Bowl denied Texas a national championship.

The national media recognized the story. *Sports Illustrated's* Doug Looney was the first to pick up on Campbell as a national figure, and it wasn't long before other high-profile national publications were calling as well.

"This is Kent Demaret with *People* magazine," one phone caller said. "And I have heard a story about some football player you have there whose mother raises roses . . . "

"Let me tell you," came the reply, stopping him in mid-sentence, "about Earl Campbell."

The week when the Heisman votes came due, the story of Ann and Earl Campbell was in every supermarket and on every magazine stand in the country. The prediction of the little media guide came true. Earl became the first Heisman Trophy winner in Texas Longhorn history.

His storied professional career created some of the most memorable plays in league history, as he ran his way into the NFL Hall of Fame.

Fred Akers, Earl Campbell, and Earl's mom, Ann Campbell, celebrate Campbell's Heisman Trophy in 1977.

It has been a long time since Darrell Royal became a father figure to him and his senior season under Akers created a year in which he won the Heisman. In some ways, the years were not kind. The pounding he took as a pro player aged his body, and as the old song says, he "don't get around much any more."

But he had carved an unmistakable legacy. Earl Campbell had shown integrity by choosing to come to The University of Texas. It was a brave young heart who played the game with reckless abandon, and who came back to earn his degree, despite being one of the most famous players in pro football.

Fame, as we have learned, is not always friendly. But in the twilight of a moment, somewhere in the memory is an incredible athlete, a running back without peer, and a young man whose Mama gave him values that will always stand the test of time.

In the recruiting season of 1995, he would use those same values to talk with another young man who was considering coming to Texas to play football. Where Campbell had come from, the Piney Woods of East Texas where his mother had raised roses, this was a savvy young man from San Diego, the city by the sea in California.

His dream was to win the Heisman Trophy, and on his recruiting visit to Austin, he would meet somebody who did. Campbell, who worked as a member of the UT athletics staff as he built his own food sales industry, was able to talk with Williams as a UT employee. They were different, Earl and Ricky, but they were alike in two things: They would be the best football players of their respective eras, and they would play for The University of Texas.

Times had changed immensely in the twenty years between Earl Campbell's run for the Heisman Trophy and the challenge that faced Ricky Williams in 1998. Where Campbell was coming off a lackluster season of injury in 1976, Williams had been the nation's leading rusher and had won the Doak Walker Award as the nation's leading running back. But when John Mackovic, the head coach when Williams was recruited, was reassigned following the 4–7 season of 1997, speculation abounded that Ricky would bolt for the NFL and forgo his senior year at UT.

Thus, Williams became the top "recruit" for new head football coach Mack Brown. If Williams decided to stay in school, Brown had a cornerstone on which to build. He was, at that point, within reach of the NCAA all-time rushing record. But it would take some managing by Brown and his staff to win enough games so that Williams would be noticed and to get him the yards he needed for the record.

In an in-depth conversation with Brown, Williams asked him, "Coach, do I do what people tell me I should do, or do I do what in my heart I want to do?"

Brown thought for a minute and then responded, "Few people in life ever get to do what they really want to do," he said. "If you need the money right now, then you should go. If you don't, then do whatever it is that you really want to do."

Brown was also struck by Williams's first question to him. It wasn't about how many times he'd get the ball or how Texas would handle his national honors campaign. It was, "Coach, can we win this year?"

When Ricky Williams announced he was returning to school for his senior year, Brown and his Longhorns had the major piece

The Unsuspecting Hero

It had been seven seasons since Texas had beaten Oklahoma in the annual Texas-OU game in Dallas, but as the Longhorns headed to the Cotton Bowl Stadium in 1977, it looked as though the annual battle of the Red River was just about a toss up.

Texas had rolled to lopsided victories over Boston College (44–0), Virginia (68–0), and Rice (72–15). The Longhorns had moved up to number five in the country. Oklahoma was also unbeaten, and the Sooners were ranked number two nationally.

The Longhorns had two quality quarterbacks—Mark McBath and Jon Aune. And with Earl Campbell in the backfield, the offense had been almost unstoppable. With the Sooners leading 3–0 in the first quarter, McBath was lost for the season with a broken ankle. But the Texas faithful didn't fret, because Aune was a popular choice as well.

On the next series, Aune stumbled over an Oklahoma lineman and tore ligaments in his knee.

Suddenly, UT's hopes rested on an untested reserve with little playing experience, a third-team quarterback named Randy McEachern. When McEachern trotted onto the field, Campbell broke away from the huddle and led his teammates in supportive applause.

And that is how Randy McEachern became a Texas legend. He led the Longhorns to a 13–6 victory over Oklahoma and went on to quarterback the team to an unbeaten regular season. Texas finished the regular season ranked number one in the country, and Campbell went on to win the Heisman Trophy.

McEachern only yielded the starting job because of injuries over the next season and a half, and he set two passing records, despite missing part of his senior season in 1978.

to a puzzle that would come together in the fall of 1998.

Ricky's numbers had gotten him into the national Heisman picture, and John Bianco, who managed Ricky's media relations masterfully, kept Ricky and all of the right statistics in front of all of the right people.

But where Campbell came across as the humble young man from East Texas, Ricky appeared California cool. First of all, he wore his hair in dreadlocks, an out-of-the-mainstream image for some of the Heisman voters and members at the Downtown Athletic Club in New York City.

It soon became apparent however, that Ricky wasn't wearing his hair that way to make some kind of statement. He wore it that way because he liked it. And in not trying to make a statement, he made a statement: that it was okay to be different.

Williams had impressed Darrell Royal's wife, Edith, when he helped her in a chance meeting at a grocery store. He had no way of knowing the gray-haired grandmother whom he had helped was the wife of Texas's most famous football figure. But when there was some concern over Ricky's appearance when he was up for the Doak Walker Award, Royal himself had called Walker and told him not to judge before he met him. When Williams and Walker, generations apart and worlds removed from each other's cultures, met, they formed a unique friendship.

Signing balls and tossing them to each other in the spring of 1998, the two had fun as Williams claimed the Doak Walker Award for 1997. No one could know that only a few weeks later, Doak would be seriously injured in a skiing accident.

At the Cotton Bowl Hall of Fame induction that May, Skeeter Walker was there to accept the award for her husband.

Ricky Williams won the Heisman Trophy in Mack Brown's first season as a Longhorn coach in 1998.
Jim Sigmon

THE HEISMAN MEMORIAL TROPHY
DOWNTOWN ATHLETIC CLUB OF NEW YORK CITY
RICKY WILLIAMS
UNIVERSITY OF TEXAS
1998

When the conversation turned to the subject of Ricky Williams, she offered, "That young man has called Doak every week since the accident."

The national media soon had the story, and the story of the kid with dreads and the all-American boy of the 1940s soon became known throughout the country. Williams asked Brown if he could break team policy and put a picture of Walker on his locker in the Longhorn dressing room, and it was allowed. A few weeks after Walker died that fall, Texas was playing Oklahoma in the Cotton Bowl in Dallas. Walker had made the stadium famous in his days as a player at SMU, and Williams asked and received permission to wear Walker's number 37 in the Longhorns game against the Sooners. Williams led Texas to victory, rushing for 139 yards on 39 carries. After the game he presented the jersey to Walker's family in the Longhorn locker room.

While all of that was going on, Brown's first season at Texas was progressing nicely. Williams had bounced back from almost a complete shutdown by Kansas State, and as the Horns headed into Nebraska to play the Cornhuskers, he was back in the Heisman hunt.

Nebraska had won forty-nine straight home games in Lincoln when Williams and the Longhorns snapped the string. The Cornhusker crowd gave Williams a standing ovation as he left the field after gaining 150 yards on 37 carries.

Williams was the frontrunner in a crowded Heisman field as Texas came to its final game of the regular season against Texas A&M. In that game, he broke the NCAA career rushing record and finished with 2,124 yards for the season, fifth best in college football history. He also eclipsed the career record of all-purpose yards.

With a professional baseball contract that he had signed out of high school, he had helped pay his two sisters' way through UT, and with his mother, Sandy, he would set up a foundation for underprivileged kids after he finished his playing time at Texas.

The Heisman portraits of Campbell and Williams and all of the other winners were moved from the Downtown Athletic Club before its doors were closed forever. The tradition, of course, continues each year at another site. Williams's career path has now taken different directions after several successful seasons in the NFL.

Time and space continue to separate The University of Texas and the two stars. Campbell's number 20 and Williams's number 34 are the only jerseys ever to be retired in Texas football. In their own ways, they were both pathfinders. We were awed by their talent, and we were thrilled by the moments they gave us.

Fourth and Inches

As he came to the line of scrimmage and surveyed the Nebraska defense in the first-ever
Big 12 Championship game, James Brown
stood at the edge of history. Or maybe, better
said, he was right smack in the middle of it.
To understand the moment, it helps to
understand the situation.

Our story begins long before that December afternoon, 1996, in the TransWorld
Dome in St. Louis. Less than three years

before, there was no league championship game, because there was no league. Texas was the linchpin of the Southwest Conference, and Nebraska had become the dominant team in the Big 8. But the college football world had been undergoing a metamorphosis that had actually begun in the summer of 1984.

That was when a lawsuit concerning television rights and who owned them was settled. For years, the NCAA had controlled broadcast television rights for its schools and had distributed appearances and money as it chose. As new networks emerged with interest in covering sports, the parent organization held fast to its right to control the medium. But its member institutions, particularly the leading football powers, saw a new opportunity for both money and exposure. The Universities of Georgia and Oklahoma led the way in a lawsuit, and when the court's landmark decision sided with them, it became open season in the television market.

ESPN was a new player in the arena, but it had been limited to showing games on a delayed basis while the NCAA apportioned games to its over-the-air network partners. When the Georgia-Oklahoma decision came down, ESPN quickly began seizing properties that brought nationwide exposure to programs such as Florida State and Miami, which heretofore had limited reach.

The College Football Association emerged as the steward of the television rights for the large conferences and independent universities, and that system worked until the University of Notre Dame saw an opportunity and grabbed it. The Irish signed an exclusive contract with NBC, thus breaking the CFA's control of college football weekend air time. Still, the CFA continued with a good coalition of conferences, so the issue was manageable.

DeLoss Dodds, who became Texas's athletics director in 1981, played a critical role in the formation of the Big 12 Conference. Susan Sigmon

But the restlessness and the positioning created a flowing stream that was not going to be denied. The dominoes began to fall in the late 1980s, and shortly after Penn State elected to join the Big Ten Conference, the musical chairs were activated.

In Austin, DeLoss Dodds was in his first decade as Texas athletics director, and he was recognized as one of the cutting-edge athletic directors in the business.

Since coming to Texas in 1981, he had watched the defection of high-school recruits from Texas to other high-profile schools around the country. Attendance at league games at Houston, Rice, SMU, TCU, and Baylor had diminished tremendously, despite relative success on the field. When Andre Ware won the

Heisman Trophy at Houston, the Cougars averaged only 28,000 fans at their home games in the Astrodome. Part of all of that, Dodds had seen, came from the turmoil caused by recruiting scandals in the Southwest Conference. But he also knew the most important figure of all: As television was becoming such a powerful force financially and exposure-wise, the area covered by teams in the Southwest Conference had only 7 percent of America's TV sets. The Big Ten had 30 percent, even without Penn State. The Southeastern Conference had 23 percent. And the Big 8, which had even lost its regional TV package, had 7 percent.

As the dollars and the exposure opportunities began to be distributed, it was clear that the SWC and the Big 8 were in trouble.

"It usually takes a crisis to cause change," Dodds would say later, and the crisis came in the summer of 1990, when Arkansas announced it was leaving the SWC for the SEC. Rumors flew that Texas and Texas A&M were right behind the Razorbacks. But when folks go shopping, they often visit more than one store, and suddenly, the schools of the Southwest Conference were shopping or, in a couple of specific cases, being shopped.

While the old guard of the SWC entertained the notion of raiding its neighbor to the north—the Big 8—the progressives were imagining what it would be like for Texas and A&M to play Alabama and Tennessee. There was even a small but powerful group that wanted to see the Longhorns as part of the Pac 10. Conversations were held between Texas and Texas Tech (which was the closest geographically) with the Pac 10. Some even considered the possibility of Texas and Texas A&M going their separate ways in different leagues, but that idea quickly was dispatched as nonproductive.

A Lot of Eyes on Texas

During the tenure of the NCAA television package, which ran from the mid-1950s through 1983, Texas was the most televised team in college football. After 1984, when the NCAA control of college football television ended, 89 percent of UT games have been on TV. Based on ratings of all games televised live, Texas has been seen by over 750 million—that's more than three-quarters of a billion—people.

Before the flame could burn in either direction—west toward the Pac 10 or east toward the SEC—politics entered the picture. The state legislature and offices even as high as the governor's and lieutenant governor's squashed the idea, out of deference to the Texas schools in the SWC that would be left behind.

Discussions of expanding the SWC included in-state schools such as North Texas and schools as far away as Louisville and as close as Tulane to the east. To the west, informal discussions included Brigham Young, which was part of the Western Athletic Conference.

The people in the Southwest Conference office made overtures to the Big 8 to form a television alliance, where the two leagues would remain intact but would negotiate a television package together. There was talk of a merger combining all of the schools, with a playoff game between the two league champs.

Dodds, however, looked beyond the money. His goal had always been to keep Texas in a position to compete for national honors in every sport. The Southwest Conference, an institution in college athletics for more than seventy-five years, was dying a slow death. Attendance was down just about everywhere except Texas and Texas A&M, and in the major sports of football and basketball, recruiting was getting harder and harder. Other schools regularly raided the football-rich arena of Texas high schools, and convincing an outstanding basketball recruit to even visit was harder and harder work.

In the Big 8, things were not a lot better. Despite the fact that both Oklahoma and Kansas had Final Four–caliber basketball programs and Missouri had a nationally respected hoops program, football was still the main attraction for television, and fact was, not many folks were being attracted.

In Texas three cities ranked among the nation's top ten in population—Houston, Dallas, and San Antonio—and the television markets in Houston and Dallas–Fort Worth were in the top ten television markets in the country. Denver, Kansas City, and St. Louis were the only cities in the Big 8 with any significant media markets at all. While the Southwest Conference had what was called a "regional" TV package that aired its league games over stations in the area, the Big 8 had not been able to generate one at all.

So when Dodds and Oklahoma athletics director Donnie Duncan got together to survey the landscape, they saw a far different future than those who wanted to hang on to what was.

In early 1994 the house of cards fell. The Southeastern Conference, which had added South Carolina along with Arkansas when Texas and Texas A&M chose not to leave the SWC, signed a five-year, $85 million contract with CBS. The network also signed one with the Big East for $50 million, effectively ending the CFA. The final crisis was at hand.

In the space of less than two months, the league that had begun as the Southwest Athletic Conference in 1915 was dismantled. Television negotiations pairing the Big 8 and SWC were virtually an afterthought for the networks, who were after new material. They found it when the Big 8 voted to invite Texas and Texas A&M and, with significant encouragement from Governor Ann Richards and Lt. Governor Bob Bullock, their respective alma maters of Baylor and Texas Tech.

Left behind were TCU, SMU, Rice, and Houston.

Texas agreed to join the merger on February 25, 1994, and on March 10 the league negotiated a television package worth $97.5 million, the most lucrative in college football history at the time, surpassing the one the SEC had cut just a month before.

The conference began play two years later, electing to split into two divisions. The North Division was exclusively former Big 8 schools, with Nebraska, Kansas, Kansas State, Iowa State, Missouri, and Colorado. In the South Division were the four former Southwest Conference schools as well as Oklahoma and Oklahoma State. And despite opposition from the coaches at all Big 12 schools, their presidents voted to have a championship game matching the division winners and sold the package to ABC-TV.

That is how James Brown came to stand with his team on the field of the TWA Dome, with less than three minutes remaining and Texas nursing an improbable lead of 30–27.

The Longhorn Hall of Honor

"In recognition of those qualities that brought credit and renown to The University of Texas," reads the plaque of members of the Longhorn Hall of Honor, which was started in 1957. Texas was one of the first universities in the country to create such an honor circle, and the organization was unique in that it considered not only success in the playing arena, but accomplishments beyond athletics as well. Thus, the name "Hall of Honor," rather than "Hall of Fame."

Members include such famous athletic figures as Roger Clemens, Ben Crenshaw, Tom Kite, Tom Landry, and Earl Campbell, as well as others such as pioneer heart surgeon Denton Cooley, a former Longhorn basketball player.

Since the league's formation, the South Division had been viewed as simply cannon fodder for the powerful North Division. There was open resentment among some media, fans, and officials in the old Big 8 toward the interlopers from the four Texas schools. So it was with a degree of irony that Texas and Nebraska, two of the winningest programs in college football, would be the first representatives of the divisions to meet to decide the first-ever championship.

Nebraska, which, along with Florida State, would be the most dominant team in college football in the 1990s, was 10–1 and within striking distance of playing for a national championship. All the number-three–ranked Cornhuskers had to do was eliminate the Longhorns, which were 21-point underdogs after winning the South Division with a 7–4 overall record.

James Brown had been a significant figure in Longhorn football. He had emerged as a hero when he got his first start and beat Oklahoma, 17–10, as a redshirt freshman in 1994. He went on to lead the Longhorns to a Sun Bowl victory that season, becoming the first African-American quarterback at Texas to start and win a bowl game.

In that 1994 season, a year that was tenuous at best for coach John Mackovic, it was Brown who effectively turned the year— and Mackovic's tenure at Texas—around as he led UT to a 48–13 win over Houston and a 63–35 victory over Baylor.

In 1995 he had piloted Texas to the final Southwest Conference championship, including a gutsy performance despite a severe ankle sprain in a 16–6 victory over Texas A&M in the league's last game ever. In leading Texas to a 10–1–1 record, he helped the Longhorns earn an appearance in the Bowl Alliance in the Sugar Bowl.

The Monday before the Nebraska game, Brown had walked into a press conference in Austin and stunned the media. Badgered by a reporter about the fact that Texas was a 21-point underdog, and "How do you feel about that?" Brown finally responded, "I don't know . . . we might win by 21 points."

In less than five minutes, it was on the national wire. "Brown predicts Texas victory."

Mackovic, who was in his fifth season at Texas, told his quarterback in a meeting that afternoon, "Now that you've said it, you'd better be ready to back it up."

The TWA Dome was packed, with a decidedly Nebraska flavor for the game that would decide the first Big 12 championship. James Brown had led his team on the field in warm-ups and was out-cheering the cheerleaders in the pregame drills.

Mackovic, who was known for creatively scripting his offense at the beginning of games, put the Cornhuskers on their heels immediately with an 11-play, 80-yard drive for a touchdown to open the game. Texas had led 20–17 at the half, but when Nebraska took its first lead of the game at 24–23 in the third quarter and then made it 27–23 with ten minutes remaining in the fourth quarter, things looked bleak for Texas.

The representatives from the Holiday Bowl in San Diego, who had come poised to invite Texas after the Horns were dispatched by Nebraska, marveled at the Longhorn Band at halftime and delivered to the Texas representatives material advertising the attractiveness of San Diego as a bowl destination site.

But four plays later, Brown hit receiver Wane McGarity for a 66-yard touchdown pass and Texas was back in front, 30–27.

Nebraska's ensuing drive stalled at the Longhorn 43, and with 4:41 remaining in the game, Texas got the ball at its own 6. A penalty on the first play pushed the ball back to the 3. Five plays later, Texas had moved the ball to its own 28 yard line. It was fourth down, with inches to go.

Mackovic called time out and summoned Brown to the sidelines. "Steelers roll left," he said. "Look to run."

Mackovic had used his weapons well in the game. He had taken Ricky Williams, who would win the Heisman Trophy two years later, and used him primarily as a decoy. Priest Holmes,

The Favorite Son

David McWilliams, who captained the 1963 Longhorn team and went on to become head coach of the Longhorns, spent more time in Texas athletics than any other person in modern history.

A three-year letterman (1961–63), McWilliams entered high school coaching following his graduation from Texas. He joined Darrell Royal's staff in 1970 and served as an assistant to both Royal and Fred Akers before taking the head coaching job at Texas Tech in 1986.

In 1987 he realized a dream when he was named head coach of the Longhorns. McWilliams led the Longhorns to a 31–26 record in five seasons, and his 1990 team won the Southwest Conference and finished the regular season ranked number three in the country. He was reassigned following a 5–6 record in 1991 but continued working in the athletics department as the executive director of the Longhorn Letter Winners Association.

who had been the third back after coming off a knee surgery earlier in his career, had been the workhorse.

Both players, of course, would go on to fame in the NFL, with Holmes becoming the league's top rusher at Kansas City. Holmes finished the game with 120 yards on 11 carries, and Williams carried only 8 times for 7 yards. Everybody had seen the pictures of Holmes as he perfected a leap over the middle of the line for short yardage. He had scored 4 touchdowns that way against North Carolina in the Sun Bowl alone. Nebraska geared to stop Holmes.

And now, there was James Brown, right where you left him at the start of this story.

"Look to run," Mackovic had said. But as the team broke the huddle, Brown looked at his tight end, Derek Lewis, and said, "Be ready."

"For what?" Lewis responded, turning to look at his quarterback as he walked out to his position.

"I just might throw it," Brown replied. Brown took the snap, headed to his left, and saw a Nebraska linebacker coming to fill the gap. He also saw something else. There all alone, 7 yards behind the closest defender, stood Derek Lewis.

Seventy thousand fans and a national television audience collectively gasped as Brown suddenly stopped, squared, and flipped the ball to Lewis, who caught it at the Texas 35, turned, and headed toward the goal. Sixty-one yards later, he was caught from behind at the Cornhusker 11. Holmes scored his third touchdown of the game to ice it at 37–27 with 1:53 left.

The next morning, Mackovic was on a plane to New York to attend the National Football Hall of Fame dinner and to accept on national TV the Fiesta Bowl bid to play Penn State. The reaction and reception he received were amazing. In choosing not to punt from his own 28, thus leaving the game in the hands of his defense with three minutes left, Mackovic had swashbuckled his way into a significant amount of fame. Had it failed, he would have been second-guessed forever, because the Cornhuskers would have had the ball only 28 yards from the goal, where a very makeable field-goal attempt would have tied the game, and a touchdown would have won it.

There is an old Texas proverb that says it is only a short distance from the parlor to the outhouse. There was John Mackovic, sitting on a stuffed sofa in the living room on CBS-TV, accepting a bid as the Big 12 representative to the Fiesta Bowl, as Nebraska dropped from national title contention and went to the Orange Bowl.

"The call" seemingly had been seen by everybody in America. Ushers at the David Letterman show were high-fiving the Texas coach, and managers of leading restaurants were sending him complimentary bottles of wine.

James Brown had made good on his promise, even if he didn't quite get the full 21-point margin. He passed for 353 yards,

James Brown making his famous fourth down pass to seal a victory over Nebraska in the first-ever Big 12 Championship game. Jim Sigmon

Derek Lewis runs with James Brown's fourth down pass. Jim Sigmon

hitting 19 of 28 passes, including the touchdown pass to McGarity. He had led Texas to a stunning victory. The mystique of the North Division of the Big 12 had been shattered, and the guys from the South had proved they belonged.

In the next eight years, Big 12 schools would play in the national championship game five times, as the young league quickly solidified itself as a true power in college football.

The victory marked the high-water mark for Mackovic, who was able to enjoy the popularity of "the call" for a short spring and summer. When Brown sprained his ankle in the season opener of 1997 and couldn't play the next week against UCLA, disaster struck. Texas came apart as the Bruins beat the Horns, 66–3. Brown never really got well, and neither did his coach. When the Texas season ended at 4–7, Mackovic was removed from the head coaching position and reassigned within the athletics department.

James Brown made a run at arena football and spent some time playing in Europe. In his time at Texas, he had earned a special place. First, he destroyed the myth that an African-American couldn't play quarterback at Texas, and second, he had taken "fourth and inches" and made it into a euphoria that will forever rank as one of the greatest moments in the storied history of Longhorn football.

Orange Roses in Pasadena

Somehow, you had to believe they had one last miracle left in them. And as the ghosts of Rose Bowls past seemed to dance in the clouds up through the foothills of the San Gabriel Mountains, more than 93,000 watched in person and millions more on television—sure enough, there it was. Never in the ninety-year history of the Rose Bowl has a game been decided on the final play. But in year ninety-one, on January 1, 2005, it was.

Throughout a week of preparation, as Texas and Michigan lived two blocks apart at swank Century City hotels right there near Beverly Hills, they had traveled different yet similar paths to this space.

From the windows facing east from the Horns' home, the Westin Century Plaza, you could see the sign on the distant hill: HOLLYWOOD—where dreams come true.

The improbable match pairing two of the nation's all-time winningest football programs for the first time and putting them in the country's most famous collegiate venue had been devised by a series of events that could have been created in a movie script.

The saga had its heroes and its bad guys, and depending on which side you were on, the characters could have easily switched places. In the final weeks of the 2004 season, the drama played out in a conglomerate known only by its initials: the BCS.

The Bowl Championship Series. Established by the commissioners of the nation's power football conferences, the BCS featured four football games played in the Fiesta Bowl in Tempe, Arizona; the Orange Bowl in Miami; the Sugar Bowl in New Orleans; and the Rose Bowl in Pasadena. Three of them, the Fiesta, Orange, and Sugar, were members of the coalition. The Rose was not, but because its television partner, ABC, was the network of the BCS, it agreed to place its hallowed game in the mix.

Under the plan, the BCS national championship game would rotate sites among the four bowls. The winners of the Pac 10 and Big Ten, which were actually co-owners of the Rose Bowl, agreed to be a part of the arrangement. The other guaranteed berths went to the winners of the Big 12, Southeastern, Atlantic

Coast, and Big East conferences. That left two at-large spots. And that is where this saga begins.

On October 9, 2004, two unsuspecting participants began a quest for one of those places. Texas and California, both unbeaten at the time, lost to Oklahoma and Southern Cal, respectively. After a controversy and a threatened lawsuit involving non-BCS conference teams, the commissioners decided that any university from those leagues that finished in the top six in the final poll would get one of the at-large bids. The rules also said that any team, BCS conference or otherwise, that finished in the top four would get an at-large bid.

In the fall of 2004, Utah, from the Mountain West Conference, was enjoying its best season in history. While Southern Cal, Oklahoma, and Auburn were busy putting together unbeaten seasons in the quest to play in the national championship game (which would be held in the Fed Ex Orange Bowl in Miami), Texas, California, and Utah were in a race for the two so-called at-large spots.

For much of the last month of the regular season, California held the fourth spot, Texas was fifth, and Utah sixth in the BCS standings. The BCS formula was made of three parts, including the Associated Press writers' poll, the USA Today/ESPN coaches' poll, and the average of selected independent computer polls.

The Longhorns' experience with the BCS had not been good. Despite being the only team in the country to be listed in every BCS top fifteen since 1999, Texas had been shut out of the New Year's elite. In 2003 they had been sixth in the final standings and lost a seeming lock on appearing in the Tostitos Fiesta Bowl when Kansas State upset Oklahoma in the Big 12 Championship game and earned the league's automatic berth. In fact, despite finishing in the BCS top ten each of the previous three years, various factors had kept Texas out of the mix.

When Utah finished its season unbeaten, it was clear the Utes would finish no lower than sixth and therefore had earned one of the two available slots. That left California and Texas in a dead heat for the only remaining at-large bid.

On November 20, Monday before the Longhorns' final regular season game with Texas A&M, Texas was fifth in the BCS poll, trailing Cal by the slimmest of margins. Ranked fourth in both of the polls but sixth by the computers, the Golden Bears had a ranking of .8504. Texas, fourth in the computers but sixth in the writers' poll and fifth in the coaches', was at .8301.

When the Longhorns beat Texas A&M, 26–13, on November 26, Texas employed the forces of emotion and logic. Coach Mack Brown emotionally implored media members who had covered the game to "vote for this team," and he urged them to get their colleagues to do the same. It was a promise he had made to his team, which had expressed to him the fear that they would again be left out of the BCS.

"I told them to keep their mouths shut and go out and win the game, and if they did, I would fight for them," he said.

The Texas media relations office worked from the logic side. They developed a chart showing the performance in several different categories of all of the top six teams and contacted sports information directors asking them to pass the information along to every coach in the coaches' poll.

If anything, Brown sensed a backlash from the media, as the Longhorns actually fell farther behind Cal in the AP poll the next

The Mack Attack

When Mack Brown came to Texas in December of 1997, he arrived with the stated purpose "to win championships with nice kids who graduate." With that, he embodied all that Texas could ask in a head coach.

Brown's teams not only won games, they also succeeded in the classroom. In his previous stop at North Carolina, 70 percent of his student athletes earned their degrees. At Texas, his teams were on pace with similar numbers.

In his first seven seasons, his teams won or tied for the South Division of the Big 12 three times and won four of the seven bowl games they attended, including the 2005 Rose Bowl in the Bowl Championship Series.

Brown's teams also established a remarkable record, winning at least nine games in each of his seven seasons, including three eleven win seasons in 2001, 2002, and 2004. At home through the 2004 season, Texas had sold out every home game after Brown's first two and had lost only three home games in seven years.

His 137 victories from 1990 through 2004 ranked as the second-most nationally among active NCAA Division 1-A coaches.

week. But the coaches were listening. On November 27, in the next-to-last poll, Texas had closed Cal's lead to an amazing margin of .0013. Cal was at .8431, and the Longhorns at .8418.

In the final twist of fate, California had one game remaining, a contest at Southern Mississippi, which was moved to the end of the season because of a September hurricane in the Gulf of Mexico. The interest in the game caused ESPN to televise it, and Cal, which as a West Coast team had experienced little national media coverage, had its chance for a showcase.

Brown's plea, and the work of the media relations staff, had accomplished one thing: It had asked the voters to "take a look." It all came down to the final day of the college football season.

Texas could only sit and wait. They had made their case—an impressive final game against archrival Texas A&M—and had made a plea for the voters to take a close look. And that day, they did.

Texas's first opening came when Southern Cal struggled, almost losing to rival UCLA, which finished 6–5. All season long, California's most notable moment was its narrow loss to Southern Cal. Fifteen minutes before Oklahoma and Colorado kicked off in the Big 12 Championship game, Southern Mississippi and California started on ESPN.

Because of the awareness created, the whole country watched. The option for impartial viewers soon disappeared as Oklahoma quickly dispatched Colorado. Now, it was up to California. And there they were, struggling with an inspired Southern Miss team trying to protect its home turf. In truth, this was not the typical Southern Mississippi powerhouse. This was a team that had become bowl-eligible the week before, was 6–4, and had been humiliated in two of its previous three games.

With a little over five minutes left in the game, Southern Miss was within 1 point. A group of Longhorn team managers made the trip to Hattiesburg, constantly holding up signs reminding voters to remember Texas. Cal went on to win, but the question was, was it enough?

A subplot of the story had been played out in conference calls and individual conversations as athletic administrators and bowl reps played "what if?" during the final week.

Under the agreements between the conferences, each league has a designated "safe place." The Tostitos Fiesta Bowl had an arrangement with the Big 12. The Rose Bowl, following a tradition that goes all the way back to the 1940s, had the representatives of the Pac 10 and the Big Ten as its anchors. The SEC's anchor was the Sugar, and the Orange generally was aligned with the Big East and ACC. When one of its anchors goes to the national championship game, that bowl gets the first pick from the at-large pair. With Southern Cal ranked number one, that meant that, under normal conditions, the Rose would get first choice for an opponent to play the Big Ten champion, which was Michigan.

But there was one more factor to be considered. Oklahoma was the number two team, and therefore the Tostitos Fiesta Bowl would lose its anchor. And since a Big 12 representative, Texas, might be an at-large team, there was a clause that would allow the Fiesta to take the Longhorns as the first at-large pick. When two teams from the same league get into the BCS and one is playing for the championship, the bowl that lost that anchor has the option of replacing it with its league brother.

DeLoss Dodds, the Texas athletics director, knew the rule well. He had been part of the foundation of the whole thing and was heavily involved when the Fiesta approached the Big 12 about an alliance. Dodds knew the options that would be available if Texas were to receive a bid. Southern Cal and Oklahoma appeared locked into the national championship game. If Auburn won the SEC, which it was heavily favored to do, it would claim the Nokia Sugar Bowl berth. Virginia Tech had won the ACC and would likely join Auburn in New Orleans. That left Utah, Big East winner Pittsburgh, and either Texas or Cal to fill two spots in the Fiesta and one in the Rose Bowl. As the Fiesta courted Texas, Dodds saw a tremendous opportunity for his team and his school. If things were to fall right, Texas could play Michigan in the Rose Bowl. It was an opportunity that would tremendously excite Texas fans. The Longhorns had never played in the Rose Bowl, and they had never played Michigan. Dodds didn't think his public would be as turned on to play either Pitt or Utah in Tempe. So as the week progressed, he lobbied the Fiesta Bowl folks to pass Texas if they were in the pool. A skilled negotiator in any setting, Dodds called in a marker from a past debt and hoped it would work in everyone's best interest.

Now it was Sunday, the day after the final games. Dodds and Brown were on their way to the National Football Foundation's Hall of Fame dinner in New York. It was a little after 3 o'clock when the Continental Airlines jet touched down at LaGuardia International Airport. The two men looked at each other as Dodds quickly turned on his cell phone and made a call. Then he leaned across the aisle and said, "We're in. You are playing Michigan in the Rose Bowl."

Texas hadn't displaced Cal in either the writers' or the coaches' poll, and the computers hadn't changed. But the Longhorns had narrowed the gap in the two human polls just enough to overtake the Golden Bears. The Longhorns had cut the lead in the coaches' poll to just five points and had a final margin in the BCS poll of .8476 to .8347.

A Message from the Past

Midseason during the 2004 campaign, Longhorn quarterback Vince Young had just gone through a couple of tough games—a loss to Oklahoma and a narrow victory over Missouri. Critical media and fans questioned whether the 6'6", 230-pound Young would eventually be moved from the quarterback position. One of the points they were concerned about was his passing technique.

The Longhorn coaches put together a film clip of Young as a high school quarterback and during successful times in his first year and a half at Texas. And they also got some great advice from a significant source.

Mack Brown keeps a book on his desk entitled *Championship Football*. It was written in 1947 by the legendary former Longhorn coach and Hall of Famer D. X. Bible.

While pundits dissected Young's throwing motion, Brown found an interesting retort in Bible's book.

"If a player throws the ball freely and accurately," wrote Bible, "a coach should not be concerned with how he holds the ball. As with all things fundamental, results count."

Following the Missouri game, Young had a breakout game against Texas Tech and went on to lead Texas to the Rose Bowl championship with an MVP game against Michigan. Six times during the final games of the season, Young brought his team from behind.

"He quit trying to change and just went back to playing the game," said Brown, "which is what we wanted him to do all along."

In his first two seasons, Young had completed 60 percent of his passes, the best ever for a Longhorn over that period.

The Fiesta Bowl had passed on Texas, and the Rose Bowl chose the Longhorns to replace the number one USC Trojans. Brown and his team, which had come from behind to win in every one of its last five games, had done it again. Longhorn fans were buying tickets at the rate of a hundred a minute, and Texas was not only making its first-ever BCS bowl appearance, it was going to the Rose Bowl.

They say it never rains on The Parade, and game day in Pasadena was no exception. Not on the Tournament of Roses Parade, and not on Texas's, either. Despite a record-setting week of rain in Los Angeles, game day and parade day dawned bright and clear. By the time Texas and Michigan kicked off, it was overcast, but the rain stayed away. And when that kickoff came, the historic stadium was an artist's canvas of the burnt orange of Texas and the blue of Michigan.

The giant B-2 Stealth bomber had put a punctuation mark on the national anthem with the second flyover of the pregame ceremonies, and now, it was time to put away all of the talk that had been about a shadowy syndicate known as the BCS. Most of that had ended when Texas Tech had soundly defeated California in the Holiday Bowl two days before. It was even appropriate that all of the history, the legends of Darrell Royal and Bo Schembechler, and the grandeur of a match between Texas and Michigan, be put aside.

January 1, 2005, in Pasadena will belong to the ages. In that space and time, in the California canyon and throughout the world of electronic media—on that grand stage—the moment also belonged to the young men on the teams of the Longhorns and the Wolverines.

It was fitting that in this first meeting of these two, in Texas's first Rose Bowl, folks were treated to what long-time observers called one of the most exciting games in the storied history of "The Granddaddy of Them All."

The day had begun for the team like any other game day, but many of their family members, along with a million other viewers from no fewer than ten live national network telecasts, watched as the Rose Parade enjoyed its fiftieth consecutive year without rain.

The trip to California had brought a unique connection between the Rose Bowl family and the Texas Longhorn family. In all of its years in bowl games, in its thirty-sixth trip over the last fifty years, Texas has never been more welcomed than it was by the Rose Bowl people. Two families, unexpectedly brought together by chance, formed a bond.

The bond of family also extended to the enormous Texas contingent that made the trip to Pasadena. From the nine charter planes that the Texas Exes brought from Texas to the thousands of Longhorn fans who gathered on the West Coast from California and other locations, it was the largest migration of a people with a common purpose in Lone Star state history. Of the 93,000 plus in the stadium, more than half were wearing burnt orange. People who hadn't been around the program in years joyously celebrated the New Year in Tinsel Town. All of that is important to this story, because the theme of the 2005 parade, and therefore the theme of the game, was "Celebrate Family." But the epicenter of the family experience was a unique group of college-aged kids and their coaches, who redefined the word "team." That is why those who had watched Texas all season expected the miracle.

They had seen it early in the season in Arkansas, when it looked for all the world that the Razorbacks were maneuvering for a victory before Texas stripped their hopes away, causing a fumble and recovering it. The circle tightened when they were down 35–7 to Oklahoma State, and again when the Horns seemingly faced certain defeat in Kansas, and yet again when a stunning play put them behind at halftime to Texas A&M. So it was to be expected that they would swap leads with Michigan, that they would somehow snatch victory from the Wolverines' determined jaws.

The experience in the Rose Bowl was a portrait of a team, its coaches, and the people behind it. From the steamy days of conditioning in the spring, through the hot Texas summer, they had worked for this moment. They had laughed together, cried together. In separate sessions with their position coaches, they had opened their souls before their teammates.

So, when Cedric Benson, the Doak Walker Award–winning running back who played with supreme toughness all season, hurt his knee when he cut on a 9-yard run to open the game, Vince Young had his back and the Texas offense adjusted.

In the traffic coming back from the media day at the Home Depot Center on Thursday, Cedric had talked about the team, and the fact that this team had made the game of football a unique blend of work and fun. Asked about the secret to the good karma, he thought for a minute and then said, "Vince Young."

Sometime after the struggle against Oklahoma and Missouri, probably in the mountains of Colorado and certainly on the South Plains of Texas against Texas Tech, this became Vince Young's team. And Saturday in Pasadena, the Longhorn junior quarterback took center stage at the most famous venue in college football.

A Rose-colored Success Story

Vincent Young came out of Houston Madison High School as one of the state's most acclaimed young quarterbacks, and in his redshirt sophomore year at The University of Texas, he certified that status.

En route to the Rose Bowl game against Michigan, Young had already put up some impressive numbers and recorded some dramatic moments. First he had brought the Longhorns from a 35–7 deficit to a stunning 56–35 victory over Oklahoma State. Perhaps his most significant moment was a game-saving play on the road at Kansas. Facing fourth down, with 18 yards to go and trailing 23–20, he scrambled for a first down. Then, with only 11 seconds left, he hit a touchdown pass for a 27–20 win.

The Rose Bowl game, however, would thrust him onto the national scene. And no one saw it coming more clearly than Greg Davis, his quarterback mentor and the Longhorns offensive coordinator.

In the coaches booth in the press box atop the storied stadium, Davis watched Young take over the football game after Michigan had moved to a 10-point lead, 31–21, at the end of the third quarter.

When Young scored a touchdown early in the fourth quarter, Davis said over the headset to the Texas bench, "I think he's trying to win this thing by himself . . . and if we give him a little help, I think he'll do it."

Young would put Texas ahead, 35–34, a short time later, with his fourth rushing touchdown of the game and then lead a game-winning drive in the final minutes of the 38–27 victory. He finished with 372 yards of total offense, 192 rushing and 180 passing, earning Most Outstanding Offensive Player honors in the game.

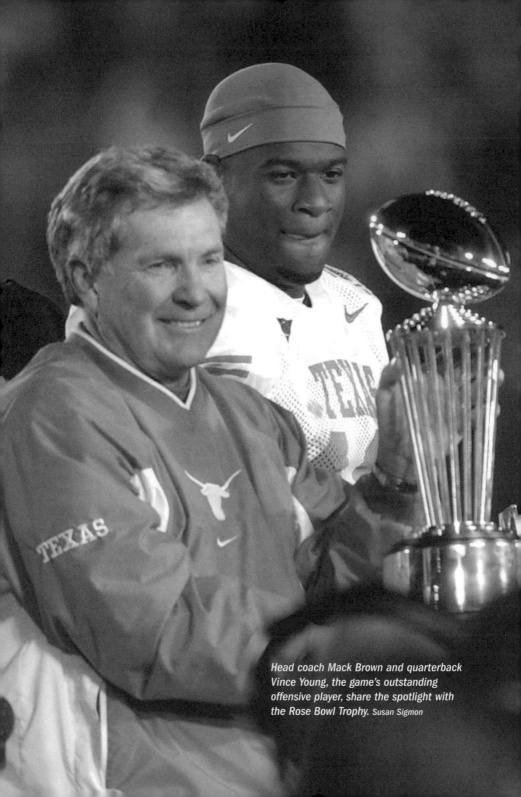

Head coach Mack Brown and quarterback Vince Young, the game's outstanding offensive player, share the spotlight with the Rose Bowl Trophy. Susan Sigmon

In the history of Texas football, there are moments that everyone remembers. There are games that define a program or, perhaps better said, define a mindset. That is what happened in Pasadena. That is why this team, which had its critics and its doubters along the way, never doubted itself.

There have been Texas teams, even recently in the Brown era, that probably had more high-profile talent. But fusion and destiny aren't built on a computer, and as we've said before, destiny makes an interesting traveling companion.

And so it was that destiny weaved its way into the Rose Bowl Stadium. Make no mistake about this: The challenge was significant. This was not your average opponent. Michigan won the Big Ten and, except for a couple of glitches along the way, was in position to contend for the national championship.

They have been to twenty Rose Bowl games in their storied history, including the first. They knew the territory, right down to the blades of grass dampened from the week's rains. And they had rare talent.

But as the folks in the ads say, "You've got questions? We've got answers." When it seemed that time was running out on Texas, the Longhorns reached down for one more reply.

And there, with only 2 seconds remaining in the game and the Horns down by 2 points, stood a senior kicker named Dusty Mangum.

So many times over the last four years, Dusty walked on the field, just as he walked onto the Texas team, and kicked the football. Mack Brown called his field goal unit around him and told them, "If you do your job and protect, he'll kick this."

Dusty Mangum celebrates his last-second field goal that gave the Longhorns a victory over Michigan in Texas's first-ever Rose Bowl game. Susan Sigmon

Twice Michigan called time-out in an attempt to play with Mangum's mind. Brown countered, laughing with him and telling him, "I wish I had the chance you have. You're gonna be a hero and win this football game. You're the luckiest guy in the world."

Finally, the moment came. The holder, Tony Jeffrey, put the ball down, and Mangum swung his right leg.

Legend will say that in a desperate effort, a Michigan player actually tipped the ball, sending the strong kick into a free flight, turning and wobbling toward the south end of the stadium, away from the canyons of the Arroyo Seco.

Call it what you will, Darrell Royal says luck is when preparation meets opportunity. Maybe that was it. Or maybe, just maybe, the Good Lord looked down on His special child and determined that Dusty Mangum shouldn't have to go through the rest of his life remembering what might have been.

Those who were there said the world seemed to go in slow motion—that the ball seemed to take an eternity to reach the goal posts. But when the two officials on either side of the goal posts stepped forward and raised their hands, the burnt orange in the stadium exploded.

The team carried Dusty off on their shoulders; they dumped ice water on Mack Brown. Equipment managers popped out Texas Longhorn Rose Bowl Champion caps, and Mangum was wearing one as he rode off into the sunset on the shoulders of his teammates. Vince Young, who scored four rushing touchdowns and passed for another, ran over to the Texas fans and then straight into a huge national spotlight. Back home in Austin, the Tower was orange, and Longhorn faithful around the world celebrated.

Late in the night, from his hotel room at the Century Plaza, Darrell Royal made a room-to-room phone call to Mack Brown. "That," he said, "is a game that will be remembered forever. They'll be talking about that one long after you and I are both gone."

What they will remember will be a special group that brought special pride, a team that played with all of its heart and its soul, and absolutely refused to lose.

And that is why you knew, you just knew, they had one last miracle left.

About the Author

Bill Little is an award winning writer who has been a part of University of Texas athletics for more than forty years. He covered UT football as a student and as a sportswriter for the *Austin American-Statesman*. He is widely recognized as the leading historian of Texas athletics.

THE INSIDER'S SOURCE

With more than 120 Southwest-related titles, we have the area covered. Whether you're looking for the path less traveled, a favorite place to eat, family-friendly fun, a breathtaking hike, or enchanting local attractions, our pages are filled with ideas to get you from one state to the next.

For a complete listing of all our titles, please visit our Web site at www.GlobePequot.com. The Globe Pequot Press is the largest publisher of local travel books in the United States and is a leading source for outdoor recreation guides.

FOR BOOKS TO THE SOUTHWEST